NEW ZEALAND BASICS 2

my history

my people

RUTH NAUMANN

NZ Basics 2: My History, My People
2nd Edition
Ruth Naumann

Cover design: Cheryl Rowe
Text design: Cheryl Rowe
Typeset: Cheryl Rowe, Macarn Design
Production controllers: Jess Lovell and Siew Han Ong
Reprint: Jess Lovell

Any URLs contained in this publication were checked for currency during the production process. Note, however, that the publisher cannot vouch for the ongoing currency of URLs.

Acknowledgements
The author and publishers wish to thank the following:
Brenda Cantell for the illustrations on pages 6, 7, 10,18, 23 and 30; Alexander Turnbull Library, National Library of New Zealand, Te Puna Matauranga o Aotearoa for the following images: page 7, Abel Tasman (ref A-044-006); page 8, Captain Cook (ref A -217-010); page 9 the Endeavour, Richard Langmaid (ref F-113204-1/2); page 11 reconstruction of the signing of the Treaty of Waitangi, Leonard Mitchell (ref A-242 -002); page 12 sketches on board an emigrant ship (ref F-661-1/4-MNZ); page 14 Heke fells the flagstaff at Kororareka, Arthur McCormick (ref A-0004-037); page 15 Potatau Te Wherowhero, first Maori king (ref F-3109-1/2); page 16, Death of Major Von Tempskey at Te-Ngutu-o-te-Manu, Kennett Watkins (ref C-033-006), page 22 bush hut (ref G-24134-1/2); page 24 frozen meat, Steffano Webb (ref G-9113-1/1); page 25 pensions, John Pascoe (ref F-456 -1/4); page 26, Kate Wilson Sheppard (ref 1/2-C -09028-F); page 27 Old age pensioners collecting social security at a Post Office (ref 1/4-000456-F); page 28 A tight corner, a New Zealander, Montbard (ref A-256-002); page 29 Boy in dog-drawn cart (ref 1/1-006229-G); page 31 'The moa and the lion', Trevor Lloyd (ref F-21875-1/2); page 32/33 World War 1 France (ref G-13097 -1/2 and ref G-13092-1/2); page 34 influenza epidemic (ref F -97380-1/2); page 35 influenza epidemic, The Press Collection, Christchurch (ref G-8542-1/1); page 36 Russell Clark and his statue of Opo (ref C-10318-1/2); page 36 Napier nurses' home (ref C-21788-1/2 and ref F-57116-1/2); page 41 Sir Ernest Rutherford (ref 1/2-050243-F); page 42 German commemorative card showing Jack Lovelock (ref MSX-2261-076); page 43 Jean Batten in the cockpit, photograph by the Sydney Morning Herald (ref MNZ-0781-1/4-F); page 44 Cobber Kain (ref PAColl-5547-011); page 44 women digging trenches (ref PA1-q-291 -57-160); page 44 Devonport primary school (ref F-111832-1/2); page 46 Edmund Percival Hillary (ref 1/2-020196-F); page 49 NZ Centennial Exhibition poster (ref Eph-E- Exhibition-1939-01); Auckland Museum Collection for photograph on page 20 (ref C17206); The estate of the cartoonist Gordon Minhinnick and the New Zealand Herald for the cartoon page 55; Peter Bromhead for the cartoon on page 56; The New Zealand Herald for photographs on pages 48, 52, 53, 65 (top) and 66 (top); Shutterstock for photographs on pages 19, 26 (bottom), 31 (bottom), 46 (bottom), 50, 60 (middle), 61 (top), 62 (middle), 63, 64, 65 (middle), and 69; Pen and Sword Books Ltd for photograph on page 32 (top); Antartica New Zealand for photograph on page 54; Sir Peter Blake Trust (photographer Christian Fevrier) for photographs on pages 57 (top) and 59; Labour Party for photograph of Helen Clark on page 60; Wellington City Council for photograph on page 61 (bottom); New Zealand Defence Force for photograph on page 62 (top); Sarah Chaussee for photographs on page 66 (bottom) and 67 (top); Tourism New Zealand for logo and photograph on page 68; World of WearableArt for photograph on page 70.

For product information and technology assistance,
in Australia call **1300 790 853**;
in New Zealand call **0800 449 725**

For permission to use material from this text or product, please email **aust.permissions@cengage.com**

National Library of New Zealand Cataloguing-in-Publication Data
Naumann, Ruth.
My history, my people / Ruth Naumann. 2nd ed.
(New Zealand basics ; 2)
Previous ed.: New House Publishers, 2002.
ISBN 978-01702-178-04
1. New Zealand—History—Juvenile literature. 2. New Zealand —History—Problems, exercises, etc.—Juvenile literature.
[1. New Zealand—History. 3. New Zealand—History—Problems, exercises, etc.] I. Title. II. Series.
993.0076—dc 22

Cengage Learning Australia
Level 7, 80 Dorcas Street
South Melbourne, Victoria Australia 3205

Cengage Learning New Zealand
Unit 4B Rosedale Office Park
331 Rosedale Road, Albany, North Shore 0632, NZ

For learning solutions, visit **cengage.co.nz**

Printed in Singapore by C.O.S. Printers Pte Ltd.
12 13 14 15 25 24 23 22

Contents

How much do you know already?

A ▷ Use the map and description to name the following.

1 Where Treaty was signed in 1840. _____

2 Modern name for old Kororareka of flagpole-chopping fame.

_____

3 Famous dolphin put this place on world map. _____

4 Auckland Harbour Bridge built over this harbour.

_____

5 America's Cup city. _____

6 Island 80 km north of Whakatane. _____

7 Where Maori won battle of Gate Pa in 1860s.

_____

8 Where Maori King's/Queen's house is.

_____

9 Head named by Cook after boy who saw

it first. _____

10 Mountain that blew up in 1886.

_____

11 World famous terraces

destroyed by 1886 eruption.

_____

12 Mountain near Parihaka.

_____

13 First National Park. _____

14 City hit by big earthquake in 1931. _____

15 New name for bay first named Murderers' Bay by Tasman. _____

16 Harbour in which *Wahine* sank in 1968. _____

17 Strait named after famous British explorer. _____

18 Gold-rush town with bar that wrecked many ships. _____

19 Boys' high school where Jack Lovelock's oak is planted. _____

20 Gold turned it from village to huge town in 1860s. _____

/20

9780170217804

B Circle the best answer to finish the following statements about Kiwi history.

1 When Anna Paquin won an Oscar for her role in *The Piano,* she was
  a 11-years-old **b** 16-years-old **c** 22-years-old.

2 The Auld Mug that New Zealand won in 1995 was the
  a Louis Vuitton Cup **b** America's Cup **c** Round the World Cup.

3 Captain Cook's ship was called the
  a *Astralobe* **b** *Endeavour* **c** *Navigator.*

4 Kate Sheppard was a leader who wanted women to have the right to
  a divorce drunkards **b** work in hotels **c** vote in political elections.

5 Pelorus Jack was a famous
  a eel **b** seal **c** dolphin.

6 Knickerbockers are
  a trousers **b** marbles **c** thieves.

7 Richard Pearse is famous for early experiments with
  a cars **b** planes **c** trains.

8 Ernest Rutherford won the Nobel Prize for
  a literature **b** peace-keeping **c** chemistry.

9 Jean Batten was a famous
  a musician **b** flyer **c** long-jumper.

10 Barbara Kendall won Olympic gold for
  a boardsailing **b** horse-riding **c** running.

11 The man who led the New Zealand Division in World War 2 was
  a Charles Upham **b** Bernard Freyberg **c** Apirana Ngata.

12 The £ sign stands for a
  a pound **b** shilling **c** penny.

13 The man who climbed to the top of Everest with Edmund Hillary was
  a John Hunt **b** Hassan Nepal **c** Tenzing Norgay.

14 Mt Erebus is on
  a Stewart Island **b** Mayor Island **c** Ross Island.

15 The Bastion Point protest took place in the city of
  a Auckland **b** Wanganui **c** Christchurch.

16 During World War 2, New Zealanders were most scared of attack by
  a Germany **b** Japan **c** Italy.

17 Abel Tasman was
  a English **b** French **c** Dutch.

18 The man who signed the Treaty of Waitangi for the Crown in 1840 was
  a James Busby **b** William Hobson **c** Samuel Marsden.

19 The war that took place from 1914 to 1918 was the
  a Boer War **b** First World War **c** Korean War.

20 The Greenpeace ship sunk by the French in 1985 was called
  a *Rainbow Warrior* **b** *Herald Victory* **c** *Daring Dove.*

/20

2

First arrivals

New Zealand was once a country of birds and no people. Because there were no big animals to eat the birds, there were even birds which couldn't fly.

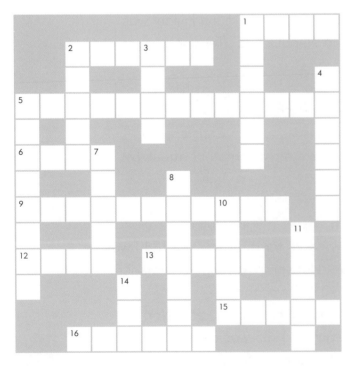

The first people to arrive here must have come from the warmer north. To the south was only the frozen Antarctica. They must have been good sailors.

These first people were Polynesians. They were Nga Tamariki A Maui – The Children of Maui. They were ancestors of the Maori. They thought of themselves as members of particular tribes. They did not call themselves Maori until much later when Pakeha, who were different, arrived. Maori meant ordinary.

The Polynesians had no written language, so nobody knows exactly when they arrived, why they came or where they came from. But they passed many legends (history stories) through generations by reciting, singing or chanting. They became tangata whenua – people of the land.

A Polynesian called Kupe is supposed to have visited New Zealand in the year 925 and sailed back home with instructions on how to get here. The Great Fleet Theory says that eight canoes came to New Zealand in 1350 and landed at different places. Tribes trace their ancestry back to these canoes. But a special scientific method called radiocarbon dating suggests that people had arrived earlier than those dates.

The homeland of the first arrivals is known as Hawaiki. Was it Hawaii or another place such as Tahiti? Did people come here on purpose or were they blown off course when visiting another island and got here by accident?

People are still puzzling over these questions.

Across

1 English for 'whenua'
2 New Zealand was much … than Hawaiki
5 Maori for 'people of the land' (7, 6)
6 Maori and Pakeha were to … each other in New Zealand
9 scientific dating method (5, 6)
12 early Polynesian voyager
13 Polynesians were their ancestors
15 direction Antarctica is to New Zealand
16 possibly where Hawaiki was

Down

1 history story
2 what a Polynesian voyaged in
3 a particular time such as a year
4 another possibility for where Hawaiki was
5 Maori for 'children'
7 early Maori thought of themselves as belonging to this
8 ancestral Maori homeland
10 New Zealand was once a land full of these
11 early Maori did not … down their history
14 before people arrived New Zealand had … big animals

9780170217804

Tasman saw New Zealand in 1642

Abel Janszoon Tasman was a Dutchman from a country called the Netherlands in Europe. He lived from 1603 to 1659.

He was an explorer, sea captain, and navigator. In those days sailors had no navigational technology. They travelled in tiny, overcrowded, wooden sailing ships. They believed in the supernatural and expected they might run into giants and sea monsters.

Abel liked his rum, had a black handlebar moustache and shoulder-length hair parted in the middle.

Although he did not set foot on New Zealand soil, Tasman was the first recorded European to see New Zealand. He had set off to discover whether there was a sea passage eastwards across the Southern Ocean to South America.

In 1642 he saw the South Island of New Zealand. He anchored in what is now called Golden Bay. But he named it Murderers' Bay because Maori in canoes rammed one of his ship's boats and killed four of the seven people in it.

The Dutch first called this country Staten Landt. They thought it might be joined to South America, which had been called Staten Landt by another explorer.

When they found it wasn't joined to South America, the Dutch called it Zeelandia Nova. This was the Latin version of the Dutch Nieuw Zeeland. Zeeland was an area in the Netherlands; nieuw means 'new'. This name became New Zealand.

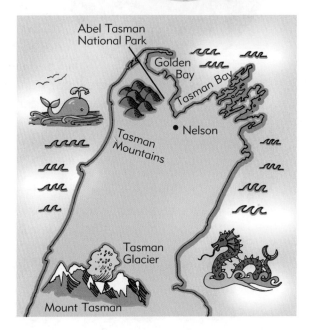

1 ▷ Fill in the gaps in the following:

a   Abel Tasman was _____ years old when he saw New Zealand.

b   Abel Tasman came from a country called _____.

c   People who live in Abel Tasman's country are called _____.

d   Abel Tasman was _____ years old when he died.

e   The names the Dutch gave New Zealand were:

_____ _____ _____

2 ▷ Places in the South Island which have Tasman's name are:

a _____   b _____   c _____

d _____   e _____   f _____

Captain Cook arrived in 1769

British explorer James Cook visited New Zealand on each of his three voyages around the world. He circumnavigated (sailed right around) both islands. He drew charts of the coastline.

Cook made his first visit in 1769, in a ship called the *Endeavour*. He kept journals and wrote notes about the Maori and their culture.

Cook 'took possession' of the country in the name of the British King. He named places he saw. For example, he named the south-west point of Poverty Bay Young Nick's Head after the servant boy who had seen it first.

Near present-day Napier, Maori canoes came up to the *Endeavour*. Some Maori tried to drag a servant off the ship into their canoe. Two Maori were killed during the rescue. Cook named this place Cape Kidnappers.

In those days, sailors used to get scurvy. It was a disease caused by lack of Vitamin C. It caused bright red spots on the skin and swollen and bleeding gums. To stop scurvy, Cook made his crew eat fruit and vegetables. The first floggings on *Endeavour* were for two sailors who ignored this order.

Cook was an excellent map-drawer. Before his visits, New Zealand was just a line on charts. After his visits, it was so well-drawn that his charts were used for a long time.

1 In the boxes on this world map, write the names of the places shown. Choose from these places – South America, Pacific Ocean, England, Atlantic Ocean, Cape of Good Hope, Africa, Australia, New Zealand, Europe, Indian Ocean.

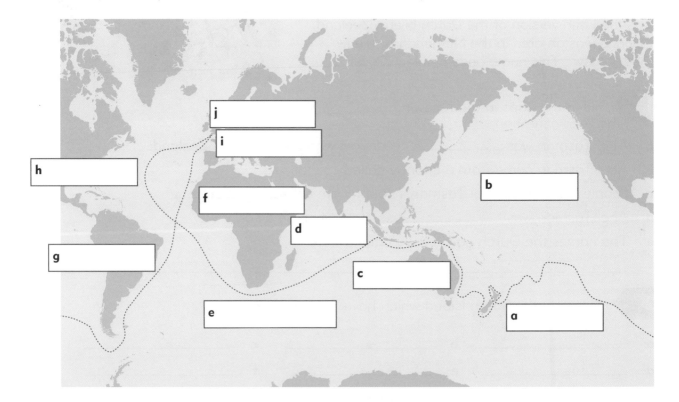

9780170217804

2 The places in the purple boxes are shown on this map of New Zealand. Write the correct names in the boxes.

New Zealand places that have
Captain Cook's name:

Mt Cook Village (Mount Cook National Park)

Cook Strait (between North and South Islands)

Cook River (South Island)

Mt Cook (South Island; also called Aoraki)

Cook's Cove (Tolaga Bay; also Bay of Islands)

Cook's Beach (Coromandel)

James Cook High School (South Auckland)

Cook's Gardens (Wanganui)

Cook Bluff (Mercury Bay)

Mount Cook National Park (South Island)

Cook Channel (Dusky Sound)

Cook Rock (Queen Charlotte Sound)

Cook's Bay (Mercury Bay)

Cook Stream (Dusky Sound)

Cook's Lookout (Mercury Bay; also Queen Charlotte Sound)

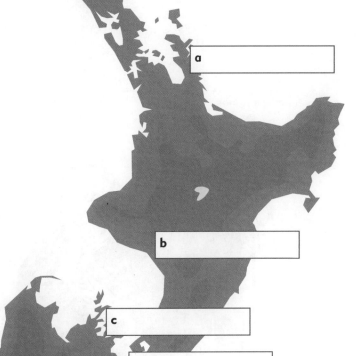

a

b

c

d

e

f

g

The *Endeavour*

Early visitors

Explorers such as Captain Cook made people in Australia, North America and Europe interested in coming to the far-off land of New Zealand. The earliest groups to visit were:

WHO	WHEN	WHY	WHERE
whalers	1790s on	to hunt whales for their oil and other products	mostly in the South Island
sealers	1790s on	to hunt seals for their skins to make felt hats	bottom of the South Island
traders	1810 on	to get kauri timber for ship masts and flax to make ropes	mostly in the North Island, especially the Bay of Islands
missionaries	1814 on	to get Maori to become Christians	mostly in the North Island, especially the Bay of Islands

a _____   b _____   c _____   d _____

Europeans and their technology led to changes in Maori society. The musket, for example, started musket wars between tribes. Thousands of Maori were killed and thousands were forced to flee their tribal areas. European diseases such as the common cold killed many Maori because they had no immunity (natural protection) to them.

Items that Maori and European swapped with each other.

muskets   nails   axes
Maori carvings
kumara   tomahawks   fresh pork
Maori mats   flax   Maori spears
blankets   kauri timber   alcohol
shrunken Maori heads   spades   fresh water

1 Label the drawings above with SEALER, WHALER, TRADER or MISSIONARY.

2 Look at the trade item boxes. Colour in green the nine items that Europeans wanted from Maori. Colour in blue the seven items that Maori wanted from Europeans.

9780170217804

The Treaty of Waitangi

By 1840 about 2,000 Europeans/Pakeha were living in New Zealand. Most were British. There were no law courts or government to stop them committing crimes. The British government had sent a special official called the <u>British Resident</u> to live in New Zealand.

He was James Busby, but he was nicknamed the 'man-o-war without guns' because he had no power.

Many other people in Britain were getting ready to come and live in New Zealand.

Britain couldn't just walk in and set up British government in New Zealand. The Maori chiefs would fight it. Britain had to make a treaty with the chiefs first. So the British government sent <u>William Hobson</u> of the British Royal Navy to make a treaty with the Maori. He sailed to Waitangi, in the Bay of Islands, because that was where the British Resident lived.

William arrived at the end of January. He lived on his ship <u>H.M.S. *Herald*</u>. He did not speak Maori so the missionaries translated the Treaty into Maori.

The Treaty was signed on 6 February 1840. This day is celebrated in New Zealand as Waitangi Day. The Treaty was signed on the lawn outside Busby's house. That house today is called <u>The Treaty House</u>.

William Hobson represented the British Crown. Many of the Maori chiefs who came to Waitangi signed the Treaty. As each chief signed, Hobson said the Maori he had learned – '<u>He iwi tahi tatou</u>'. It meant 'We are one people'. The Treaty then went around New Zealand so other chiefs could sign it if they wanted to. Not all did.

There are several versions of the Treaty. Because they are in two different languages – Maori and English – there have been different ideas about what the Treaty said exactly.

The <u>Treaty of Waitangi</u> is very short. It has only three points. They are about governing, land and rights and duties.

1 Picture study at right.

   a What treaty is being signed? _____

   b What is the name of the man who has no hat and is shaking hands? _____

   c What Maori words will he be saying? _____

   d Who are the people sitting on the ground in front of the tables? _____

   e Which flag hanging up is the same as the ones on the tables? _____

   f What sort of clothes are the Maori wearing?

   _____

   g What sort of clothes are the British wearing?

   _____

2 In the box at the end of the paragraphs, write a meaning for the underlined term in that paragraph.

The arrival of European settlers

Thousands of people from Europe, especially England, Ireland, Scotland and Wales, came to live in New Zealand after the Treaty of Waitangi was signed. Many of them settled in places that are today's big centres – Wellington, Auckland, New Plymouth, Wanganui, Nelson, Dunedin and Christchurch.

New Zealand drew these settlers because it offered them the chance to have a better life. They might even buy their own land, something they could never do at home. When they left family members behind, they knew they would probably never see them again. They were called immigrants because they were immigrating (coming to live in another country).

The voyage in sailing ships took about four to six months. The ships were crowded and leaked. Seasickness and outbreaks of disease killed many, especially children. On one ship in 1842, 65 children died. Because lanterns and candles were used on board instead of today's electricity, there was always the danger of fire. Terrible storms could cause shipwrecks.

When the early settlers landed in New Zealand, they found no houses or towns, and no roads, just bush and swamps. They had to live in tents, under tarpaulins or camp on the beach until they could build a raupo hut or small cottage. Their clothes were not always suited to the hard work they had to do. Females, for example, wore long skirts. Maori swapped food for European goods such as shirts or axes.

Children could run around barefoot. They wore clothes fashioned on what adults wore. They had to go to church but often did not go to primary school. Some children as young as eight or nine had to go out to work on farms or in rich people's houses as servants to earn a little money. There might be twelve or even more children in a family although many children died of diseases such as whooping cough. But New Zealand was a great adventure. There were no dirty industrial towns like those in Britain.

9780170217804

1 Colour in the following on the map:

RED for the continent from which Europeans came
BROWN for the countries from which British immigrants left
GREEN for the country (New Zealand) to which immigrants came
YELLOW for the continent that has the cape that immigrant ships sailed around
BLUE for the three oceans that immigrant ships sailed.

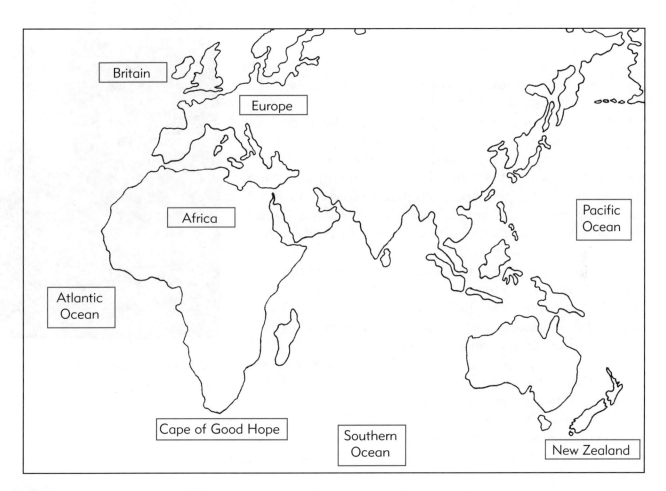

Britain

Europe

Africa

Pacific
Ocean

Atlantic
Ocean

Cape of Good Hope

Southern
Ocean

New Zealand

2 Put a tick or a cross in each box to show whether the sentence is true or false.

a Immigrant children often spent more time at Sunday School than at primary school. ☐

b Immigrants are people who go to live in a country in which they were not born. ☐

c The voyage from Britain to New Zealand took between 40 and 60 days. ☐

d Some immigrants came from Scotland. ☐

e The voyage to New Zealand held many possible dangers. ☐

f Immigrant children had a life free of responsibilities. ☐

g No immigrants went to live in the South Island. ☐

h Some harbours were dangerous and so the big centres grew up inland rather than

near the coast. ☐

Hone Heke and the flagpole

After the signing of the Treaty of Waitangi the first official flagpole with the British flag on it was put up on Maika Hill at Kororareka (Russell) in the Bay of Islands.

A Ngapuhi chief called Hone Heke from the Bay of Islands decided to protest against the flagpole. He thought the British flag was taking away the mana (authority, influence) of the chiefs and showing that New Zealand was becoming too British. He thought the chiefs were equal with the British Queen so their flag should be flying alongside. He saw the flag as a sign that British settlers were buying too much land from the tribes. He was also angry that the government and capital had shifted down to Auckland because it took trade away from the Bay of Islands. Since the flagpole had neither blood nor bones, it would not feel pain when it was cut down.

In 1844 one of Hone Heke's followers chopped the flagpole down. Twice more the British put up replacement flagpoles and Maori chopped them down. Then the British put up a new flagpole and covered the lower six metres of it with iron. The Maori chopped it down too.

When fighting broke out between British troops and Maori, the town of Kororareka got wrecked. This led to a war in the north between British troops and Heke. Some other Maori fought on the side of the British troops.

Hone Heke was helped by a chief called Kawiti who was good at engineering. He made changes to the old Maori pa to make them stronger. The war lasted a few months and Maori had several victories. The Governor decided to make peace with Heke.

In 1857 a son of Kawiti organised a group of Maori to make a new flagpole to show they were at peace with the British Queen. It was a very special flagpole and nobody ever chopped it down in anger.

1 Underline four reasons given on this page why Hone Heke attacked the flagpole.

2 Write the events from the box below in the order in which they happened into the circles on the history road.

Peace in north   Maori cut down flagpole   Kororareka wrecked   First flagpole put up
Kawiti's son organises new flagpole   War in north   Treaty of Waitangi

START

FINISH

9780170217804

The first Maori King

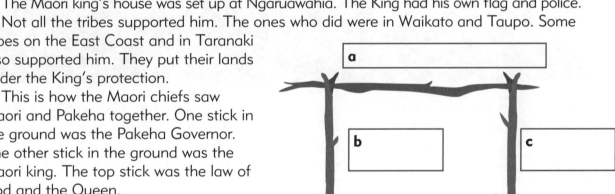

In the 1850s some Maori decided they should elect a Maori king. The Maori king would help keep the mana of the chiefs. He would try to unite all the different tribes. The Pakeha had their own government, but there were no Maori in Parliament and not many Maori qualified to vote.

The man chosen to be the Maori king was a Waikato chief called Te Wherowhero. He was crowned at Ngaruawahia in 1858. He took the name of Potatau. His family was connected to the leaders of the main ancestral canoes. He was a great warrior. His father was a famous tohunga (priest or expert) and his tribal area had the mighty Waikato River and the famous Taupiri Mountain. It was a central place for other tribes to visit. It had kai moana and food from rivers, land and bush.

Potatau

The Maori king's house was set up at Ngaruawahia. The King had his own flag and police.

Not all the tribes supported him. The ones who did were in Waikato and Taupo. Some tribes on the East Coast and in Taranaki also supported him. They put their lands under the King's protection.

This is how the Maori chiefs saw Maori and Pakeha together. One stick in the ground was the Pakeha Governor. The other stick in the ground was the Maori king. The top stick was the law of God and the Queen.

a

b

c

1 Write labels on to the drawing of the sticks.

2 Underline or highlight six reasons on this page why Maori chose Te Wherowhero as king.

3 Underline or highlight six reasons on this page why Maori chose Te Wherowhero as king.

4 Fill in the missing kings, queens or dates.

Time line of Maori kings and queen

1858 King:	Potatau
1860 King:	Tawhiao
1894 King:	Mahuta
1912 King:	Te Rata
1933 King:	Koroki
1966 Queen:	Te Atairangikaahu
2006 King:	Tuheitia

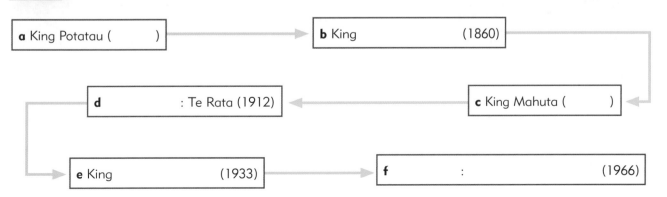

a King Potatau (   ) → **b** King   (1860)

d   : Te Rata (1912) ← **c** King Mahuta (   )

e King   (1933) → **f**   :   (1966)

The 19th century land wars

The wars between Maori and British/government troops that broke out in 1860 are often called 'Land Wars'. This is because although there were several reasons for the wars starting, one of the main reasons was land.

By 1860 there were more Pakeha than Maori in New Zealand. Pakeha wanted to buy land from Maori to make farms. They wanted to cut down bush and plant seed to grow grass for farm animals. Many Maori were worried that so much land had already been sold cheaply. Maori individuals did not own land as Pakeha individuals did. Maori tribes owned land together. This meant all the tribe had to agree to sell a block of land. Trouble started when some of the tribe wanted to sell and some did not.

The wars were fought in the middle of the North Island – in Taranaki, Waikato, Bay of Plenty and the East Coast. Some Maori fought on the British side. They were called kupapa or 'friendlies'. To start with, British troops were used. When the British troops pulled out, the troops left fighting were called government troops.

Maori had double-barrelled shotguns. The warriors were clever and fast, knew the land, and built strong pa. They were part-time fighters. Some women also fought.

The British had Enfield rifles and bayonets. They built blockhouses (small forts) and saps (trenches approaching pa) for their soldiers. They were professionals, well-drilled and experienced. They had more manpower than the Maori did.

At the battle of Orakau, when the Maori fighters had nothing to eat but raw potatoes and only wooden bullets for their guns, the British general invited them to surrender. One of the chiefs told him: 'E hoa, ka whawhai, tonu ahau kia koe ake, ake.' ('Friend, I shall go on fighting you for ever and ever.') At the battle of Gate Pa near Tauranga, about 250 Maori warriors defeated over 2,000 British soldiers.

The wars ended in 1872 when the Maori leader Te Kooti escaped into the King Country.

The government punished the Maori tribes who had fought against them. They called these Maori 'rebels' and confiscated thousands of hectares of their land.

9780170217804

1 Beside each description write either PAKEHA, GOVERNMENT or MAORI to show which group the description fits.

a the majority group in New Zealand by the 1860s _____

b wanted to buy land for farms _____

c wanted to keep hold of their tribal lands _____

d owned land as individuals _____

e owned land as tribes _____

f had kupapa fighting on their side _____

g won the battle of Gate Pa _____

h had a leader called Te Kooti _____

i built blockhouses _____

j built pa _____

k built saps _____

l called the other side 'rebels' _____

m had land confiscated from them _____

2 Complete the map.

a Write TARANAKI, WAIKATO, BAY OF PLENTY, and EAST COAST in the boxes to show where they are.

b Colour these four areas red.

c Colour the rest of the North Island green.

Clue = names follow order of boxes

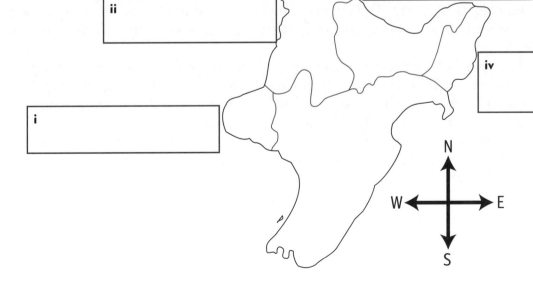

Gold rushes in the 1860s

In the days before big gold-mining companies took over, whenever someone discovered gold in a new place, people from all over the world rushed there. This was called a gold rush. New Zealand had some gold rushes in the 1860s. Most were in the South Island, away from the wars in the North Island.

The Otago Council offered a reward for the discovery of gold in their area. An Australian miner called Gabriel Read spent ten hours at the Tuapeka River in 1861 with a knife and a tin dish panning for gold. He won the reward when he saw gold shining like stars on a cold, frosty night. Thousands of miners rushed to Otago. The sleepy village of Dunedin was suddenly a wild shantytown. It grew to become a rich town with more people than Auckland.

The Tuapeka rush was followed by bigger rushes to the Cromwell, Arrowtown and Queenstown areas. Then came the West Coast gold rush which turned Hokitika into a boom town, and then a rush to the Thames/Coromandel area in the North Island.

Goldmining was hard work. The Central Otago climate froze boots and people. As miners trudged past skeletons, they saw what might lie ahead for them. There was hardly any wood to start a fire to cook food. Flooded rivers frequently swept miners away. Women who arrived in a shantytown were snapped up and married within a few days.

The West Coast was just as tough. The Hokitika bar wrecked ships. Miners had to fight rain, thick bush, sandflies, mosquitoes and fast rivers.

The rushes drew people from different parts of the world and some stayed. Several thousand Chinese came to rework the older fields especially in Otago. Their working and living conditions were terrible. Not many miners got rich. Often it was other people who

9780170217804

made money from the gold rushes. Farmers sold food to miners, storekeepers sold provisions, publicans sold alcohol and banks got more business. Industries such as clothing, flour milling and transport operators also did well.

The gold rushes were good for New Zealand because gold was something that could be exported to earn money. One Coromandel mine outdid all others by itself in the country. This was the Martha Hill mine at Waihi. It produced 35 million ounces of gold and silver between 1882 and 1952.

1 Unravel the words to make words that fit the clues.

CLUES	**WORDS**
a what the Hokitiki bar was for ships	S U G A R N O D E
b did well from gold rushes	R E S T I N S U I D
c a gold rush area	W A R N O R T O W
d place of rough huts and tents	W A N T S T H O N Y

2 Look at the map of past gold mines in the Coromandel Peninsula.

a Write in the boxes the names of the places shown. Starting from the top and moving down and around clockwise the names are: Colville, Kuaotunu, Whitianga, Pauanui, Whangamata, Golden Cross, Waihi, Paeroa, Thames, Coromandel.

b In the bottom left box set into the map, write a) the name of the place where the biggest mine was, and b) the number of mines in the Coromandel.

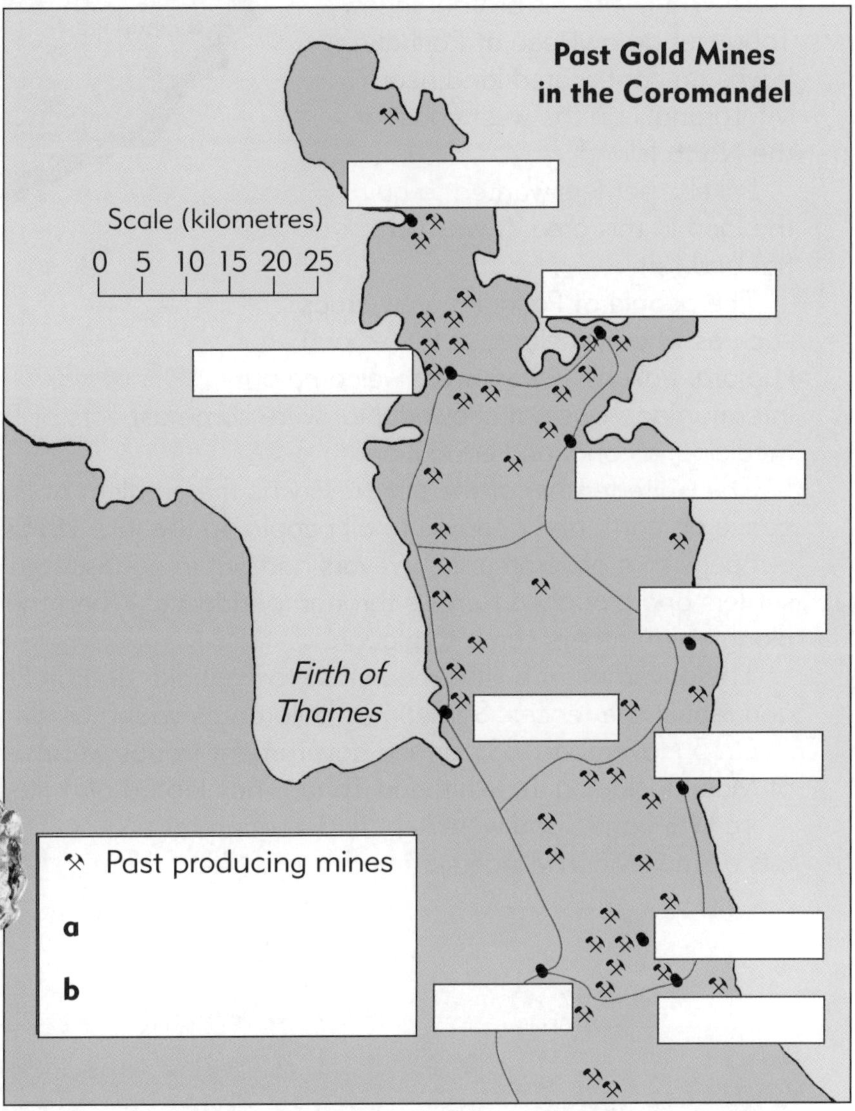
Past Gold Mines in the Coromandel
Scale (kilometres)
0 5 10 15 20 25
Firth of Thames
Past producing mines
a
b

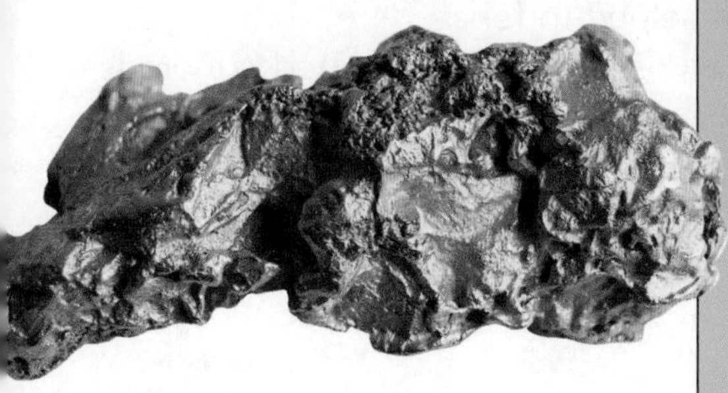

The story of Parihaka

Tim Finn's song about Parihaka tells the story of Te Whiti. He was a Maori leader who used passive resistance against the government in the late 19th century. Passive resistance means using non-violent ways to protest against something.

The Taranaki chiefs had not signed the Treaty of Waitangi. In the wars of the 1860s they fought to keep their land. The government punished them for being 'rebels' and confiscated thousands of hectares of their land.

Te Whiti, with his brother-in-law Tohu, set up a village at Parihaka. It was on confiscated land near Mt Taranaki on the west coast of the North Island.

Pakeha settlers wanted to buy the land in this area. It was rich, flat and fertile.

The people at Parihaka grew crops such as wheat, melons, potatoes and kumara. Pakeha visitors were welcome but intermarriage was not allowed. Nor were some aspects of Pakeha culture such as European medicine, alcohol and education.

The white feather of the albatross was the emblem of Parihaka. It stood for glory to God, peace on earth and goodwill to all people. In the late 1870s, Parihaka people began to pull out pegs that government surveyors had put in confiscated land. They went to the farms of settlers and ploughed furrows through paddocks. When the government arrested the ploughmen, others came to plough.

The government built a road close to Parihaka and broke down fences. Maori went out and rebuilt the fences. Sometimes children as young as six helped to fence.

On 5 November 1881 armed government troops went to Parihaka. They arrested hundreds of Maori including Te Whiti and Tohu. They looted and destroyed the houses and crops.

Te Whiti and Tohu were kept in detention for a year. Then Te Whiti rebuilt Parihaka. Today it is a small Maori village surrounded by Pakeha farms.

9780170217804

1 Put the following events into the order that they happened. Show the order by writing the letters in the boxes.

a Parihaka ploughmen ploughed up the farms of settlers.

b The government confiscated land from Taranaki tribes.

c Te Whiti rebuilt the village at Parihaka.

d Te Whiti set up a village at Parihaka.

e Taranaki tribes fought the government to try to keep their lands.

f Government troops arrested Te Whiti and Tohu.

☐ ☐ ☐ ☐ ☐ ☐

2 Look at the drawing of Parihaka ploughmen being arrested on a settler's farm in 1879 and fill in the gaps in the following sentences.

a The farm was on land _____ from the Maori by the government.

b The two animals used to pull ploughs were _____ and

_____.

c The other animal in the drawing is a _____.

d The name of the big mountain near the farm would be _____.

e The government troops would have ridden out from the town of

_____.

f The seated Maori would have walked from the village of _____.

g This event took place _____ years before Parihaka was destroyed.

In the 1870s thousands of people from Europe came to New Zealand. For many the big attraction was that they could own a farm. About the only land left to make into farms was the thick forest in the lower North Island.

When the people from Europe saw this forest they soon realised that making their farms was going to be a lot harder than they had been led to believe. They said the undergrowth was so dense a dog could run over the top of it; they said trees such as totara and rimu made the forest dark and scary. How were they to chop down such giants with only axes, crosscut saws and mattocks (picks with big blades)?

The first job was to make a small clearing, perhaps put up a tent and build a rough timber log hut with a kitchen and a bedroom. Oiled calico made windows and stamped-down dirt made the floor. The roof was made from fern, sometimes covered with canvas. A big fireplace at one end was the oven. The creek was the bathroom.

Then the rest of the forest had to be cleared. Men chopped down the huge trees. Women and children hacked at the small trees and undergrowth. Soon everybody had to wrap rags around blistered hands. Work was slow.

The chopped trees were left to dry so they could be burned later. Grass seed was sown in the ash. Cattle were put in to stop the undergrowth growing again. Paddocks were made with wooden post and rail fences. It took a week or so to dig out a tree stump. Some were too big to dig out. Often the men had to go with a work gang to clear forest for roads and railways and earn money to keep the family going. Women had so much work to do they had to get up at daybreak. Children did not go to school. They learned by doing jobs and having responsibilities.

These settlers faced many dangers – fires getting out of control, bush rats attacking babies, children getting lost in the forest, accidents, drowning in the many rivers without bridges. Doctors were too far away and too expensive. Needle and thread sewed up cuts, cobwebs were packed into wounds to help heal them, koromiko leaves were chewed to settle stomachs. Old flour bags made clothes; grass tied to a stick made a broom. The lead that tea was wrapped in was boiled and poured into moulds to make bullets for the rifle. The forest gave food – wild pork, bush honey, eels, water, berries, fern root, birds. 'Shanks's pony' (walking on your own two feet) was the transport. A cow might be trained to carry a pack until the family could afford to buy a horse.

9780170217804

1 Write in the late 19th century version of the following.

a microwave _____

b glass window _____

c iron roof _____

d wooden floor _____

e chainsaw _____

f school _____

g barbed wire fence _____

h bathroom _____

i car _____

j doctor _____

k label clothes _____

l vacuum cleaner _____

2 Finish the drawing by writing words from this unit into the gaps each box. Add colour to the drawing.

b _____ roof

f one room for _____

c _____ for window

d _____ walls

a _____ for cooking

g one room for _____

e _____ floor

h _____ for food

l _____ for drinking

j _____ for food

i _____ for food

m _____ for food

k _____ for bathroom

Refrigeration

In 1882 the 1,320-tonne sailing ship SS *Dunedin* sailed from Dunedin, New Zealand to London, England. The vessel had started life as a ship carrying immigrants. Now her specially built freezing chambers held pig, mutton and lamb carcasses, sheep tongues, kegs of butter, and a few hams, rabbits and turkeys. New Zealand's small population could not eat even a tiny percentage of the sheep grown for wool. So the idea was to see if the meat could be carried all the way to England and sold there.

The crew had a bad time in the tropics. The heat and still air made it hard to keep air circulating to keep the freezer going. They were scared that the sparks set off by the freezer would start fires. The sails did get a lot of holes burned in them but luckily the masts did not catch fire.

The trip lasted 98 days. When the ship arrived in London the frozen meat was taken to Smithfield market that night to be sold the next day. The shipment sold for double what it would have sold for in New Zealand.

This success changed the type of sheep raised in New Zealand from mainly Merino to crossbred sheep with better meat value. Farmers could now make more money from sheep by selling both wool and meat. Smaller farms could make enough to support a family.

The export of frozen meat developed so quickly that within ten years New Zealand had 17 freezing works. They could handle 3.5 million carcasses a year. London became New Zealand's biggest market.

The *Dunedin* did nine more voyages before she was lost in 1890 on the home voyage. She probably ran into an iceberg off the Cape of Good Hope.

Across

1 product sold to another country to earn money
3 compartments like those on SS *Dunedin*
6 export meatworks or abattoir (place where animals are killed) (8, 5)
10 city in England
12 first New Zealand refrigerated ship
13 sheep and pig products
14 SS *Dunedin* was this type of vessel (5, 4)
16 turned into solid ice
17 area of the earth lying in the region of the equator

Down

2 this one lasted 98 days
4 place where products are sold
5 threatened the sails and masts
7 keeping products cold and therefore fresh
8 became New Zealand's main frozen meat market
9 London's big meat market
11 carried in kegs
15 farm animal

Tarawera and White Island

Mt Tarawera is in the middle of a volcanic belt in the North Island. It suddenly erupted in 1886. The blast made a 6 km gash on the mountain top. Even people a long way off told of violent quakes to their houses, the sky full of forked lightning, a big fire roaring upwards, the earth shaking and reeling every few seconds, dense smoke, a strong smell of sulphur, a downpour of stones, mud and water, showers of ash for hours, and darkness until noon.

a

b

c

e

f

d

g

People in Auckland thought it was a warship run aground on the Manukau bar. People as far away as Christchurch could see that something bad was happening.

The eruption killed over a hundred people. A schoolmistress was dug out alive but three of her children were found dead beside her.

The eruption poured mud and stones all over Te Wairoa village. It is called 'The Buried Village' today. No trace was found of Te Ariki village. It and its people were buried under thick mud and ash.

Near Tarawera were the Pink and White Terraces. They covered several hectares and had hundreds of basins. There was nothing like them anywhere else in the world. Many tourists came to see and bathe in them. The eruption of Mt Tarawera destroyed the terraces.

Ash on the paddocks meant there was no grass for animals to eat. Children collected ash in matchboxes to sell as souvenirs.

White Island is about 80 km north of Whakatane. Its Maori name is Whakaari. It has an active volcano. In 1914 there was an explosion. All ten workers at the sulphur plant on the island were killed. The only survivor was one of the three cats the men kept at their camp. Wreckage of the men's camp and sulphur plant washed up on mainland beaches. No bodies were found. They may have been buried or blown into the sea or swept out to sea in the stream of boiling mud.

1 Fill out this chart.

	TARAWERA	**WHITE ISLAND**
Year of eruption		
Number killed		
Damage to property		

2 On the map write the names of the following places mentioned on this page.

a the island's English name

b the island's Maori name

c the big town 80 km from the island

d the mountain

e The Buried Village

f the two terraces

g the untraced village

Women were allowed to vote

In the 19th century Britain set up a parliament for New Zealand, however, only men were allowed to vote for it. The idea was that politics was the business of men while running homes was the business of women. Some, though not all, women thought that was not fair. Their leader was Kate Sheppard. They began to write and talk about women getting the vote too. They held public meetings. They said women should be allowed to have a say about who got into parliament because parliament passed laws that affected women. They also said the minds of women were just as good as those of men so women should be trusted to vote wisely.

These women were called 'suffragettes'. Suffrage means to have the vote. Another word for vote is franchise.

Some people said if women got the vote women would talk about politics instead of cooking and cleaning. Husbands and wives would have fights over politics. Women would become unfeminine. Other countries would laugh. New Zealand would not be able to borrow any more money from London. When women went to the voting polls, people would boo them. Women would vote to make New Zealand 'dry' and this would mean men could no longer go into hotels for a drink.

New Zealand women kept asking parliament for the vote. They did not have to use violence. Women in Britain did; they went on hunger strikes, chained themselves to public buildings, set fire to mail boxes, broke windows. One woman killed herself by jumping in front of the horses at a horse race.

New Zealand women got the vote in 1893. None of the awful things that people said would happen, happened.

The US state of Wyoming had given women the vote a few years earlier. But New Zealand was the first country in the world to give women the vote. Australian women got the vote eight years later in 1901.

1 ▶ Put one letter in each box to make a word about women getting the vote.

- [ ] 1st letter of surname of famous suggrogette leader
- [ ] 2nd letter of word meaning to have the vote
- [ ] 1st letter of another word for vote
- [ ] 3rd letter of what people said women would become if they got the vote
- [ ] 2nd letter of word meaning a place with no hotels
- [ ] 1st letter of country that gave women the vote in 1901
- [ ] 7th letter of first US state to give women the vote
- [ ] 4th letter of group of people who got the vote in 1893
- [ ] 10th letter of body who gave women the vote
- [ ] 5th letter of what was thought to be men's business
- [ ] 2nd (and 5th) letter of first country to give women the vote

a The word I made is _____

b It means _____

9780170217804

17 Old age pensions

All through the 19th century people in New Zealand who were poor, sick or old had only charity or their families to turn to for help. There was the idea that if you were helpless, it was somehow your own fault.

Slowly new ideas started up. Some people began to think that government had a duty to help people in need. One of these new ideas was Old Age Pensions.

A pension is a regular payment of money by government to a special group of people, such as the elderly. People who wanted the government to pass a law giving old people pensions said it was the old who had worked hard in the past to make New Zealand a good country; now it was pay-back time. People who were against the idea said it was too risky. They claimed it would ruin New Zealand and make it bankrupt.

Parliament debated the topic. In 1898 it sat for 90 straight hours while 1,400 speeches were made. The Premier (today called the Prime Minister) Richard Seddon made 147 of them. Finally the Old Age Pensions Act was passed.

At this time New Zealand's money was in pounds rather than dollars. A pound was equal to about two dollars. The pension gave 18 pounds a year to people of 65 years and over. They could only get it if their annual income was not over 34 pounds and they did not own property worth more than 50 pounds. They had to be of good character. They had to have led a 'sober and respectable life' for the past five years. They had to have a hearing before a magistrate in the Old Age Pensions Court. They had to have lived in New Zealand for at least 25 years. Asian people could not get it. Many Maori were unable to get it because they had no birth certificate to prove their age. Some had shares in tribal land which disqualified them even though they might not get any money from the land.

Old Age Pensions helped start the idea of social welfare being government giving help from the cradle to the grave. It helped make New Zealand a world leader in social welfare. Other pensions were added later such as pensions for widows with young children, for miners disabled by dust disease, and for the blind.

1 Put a tick or a cross into the boxes to show whether or not the following people would have qualified for the pension in 1898.

☐ **a** Chou is 68 and arrived from China in 1888.

☐ **b** Mere is Maori and has no birth certificate although her family say she is 75.

☐ **c** Normie arrived from England in 1890, is 66 and owns property worth 700 pounds.

☐ **d** Cyril, born in New Zealand, is 70 and was let out of jail two months ago on the grounds of ill-health after being imprisoned for fraud.

☐ **e** Sarah, born in New Zealand, is 73 and refuses to go into the Old Age Pensions Court for a hearing.

☐ **f** Eliza, born in New Zealand, is 67, has an annual income of 15 pounds through investments, and owns no property.

☐ **g** Samuel, born in New Zealand, is 69, is retired and owns property valued at 20 pounds.

The Boer War of 1899–1902

Boers were descended from Dutch people who had left the Netherlands and gone to South Africa to live. Britain claimed the land where the Boers settled. The Boers did not want to live under British rule. In 1899 war broke out in South Africa between the British and the Boers.

New Zealand was the first British colony to send troops to help Britain. Australia and Canada also sent troops.

The New Zealand soldiers fought in South Africa under the control of the British. The British paid their wages. New Zealand paid the cost of transport and gear. It was the first time that New Zealand soldiers had fought outside New Zealand as New Zealanders. They began to see differences between themselves and the British. They were generally bigger than the British. They were better riders. They got the nickname of Rough Riders because they were such good scouts and could sleep rough.

Many New Zealanders didn't know where South Africa was but they were excited about the war. School students raised money for it. They were very proud of their soldiers.

Many Boers were part-time soldiers. They had to work on their farms as well as fight. The British burned the farmhouses of the Boers. They put Boer children and women into concentration camps. The Boers had to give in.

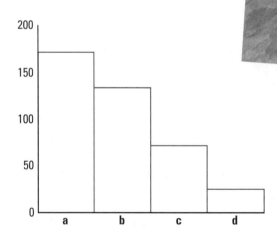

New Zealand sent 6,500 men to the war. 70 were killed in action. 25 were killed in accidents. 133 died of disease. 166 were wounded.

New Zealand doctors, nurses, and vets also went to South Africa. A group of teachers from New Zealand taught Boer children who were locked up in the British concentration camps.

1 This graph shows what happened to New Zealand soldiers who were killed or wounded in South Africa. Write in the boxes what each box stands for.

(Bar graph with y-axis labelled 0, 50, 100, 150, 200 and x-axis labelled a, b, c, d)

2 In the boxes beside the following sentences, put either **O** or **F**. **O** stands for OPINION which is something that people believe but may not be true or proved. **F** stands for FACT which is something that is true and can be proved.

- **a** New Zealand was the first British colony to send troops to the Boer War.
- **b** New Zealand troops should never have been sent to the Boer War.
- **c** In South Africa the New Zealanders got the nickname Rough Riders.
- **d** Too many troops were sent from New Zealand to the Boer War.
- **e** The British had no right to set up concentration camps for the Boers.

Life in the 19th century

In 19th century Britain, children were 'to be seen but not heard'. In New Zealand they had more freedom. Often they had adult jobs to do.

Those children 'lucky' enough to go to school faced dangers on the way. Rivers might flood. Wild pigs might charge. Their horses might buck them off. Bicycles didn't arrive until late in the century, cars until the end of the century. Both were useless out of town because of the terrible mud roads.

At school, children did their work on slates with a special pencil. They learned by chanting things after the teacher. In town there might be 100 pupils in one class. Teachers used the cane and strap to keep discipline.

Children played games such as knucklebones, hopscotch, marbles, tag, rounders and rope skipping. Indoor games included blind man's buff, hunt-the-slipper and treasure hunts. Old socks rolled up and sewn together made balls for sports. Toys were often home-made. Special toys were spinning tops, hoops, dolls, kaleidoscopes and tin wind-up toys.

Sometimes a community organised a special sports day or a picnic. At the beach, children might be allowed to take off their boots and have a paddle.

People liked listening to bands. Many girls learned the piano and musical evenings were often held in town homes. Boys got in trouble for using shanghais (catapults) or shooting guns at rabbits too near town.

Most houses were small, uncomfortable and crowded. With maybe 12 children in the family, bedrooms were shared. Sick or hurt children might die while a parent was walking or riding to find a doctor. Young children were left in charge of younger ones.

There was no electricity. Richer people had servants. Sometimes travelling salesmen visited. It might be a dentist, photographer or knife-sharpener.

Newspapers were used as wallpaper and toilet paper. The toilet was a long-drop in a small shed in the backyard. In towns a night cart might collect the sewage. It was dumped out of town, or sold to farmers for fertiliser.

Clothes were hand-made. Girls wore boots and stockings, long skirts and pinafores. Boys wore boots and stockings, knickerbockers and braces, shirts and jackets. On wash day clothes were washed at the creek or boiled up in a copper. Washing could be a whole day's work. So could the family's bath day.

> **Knickerbockers** = short breeches (trousers) gathered at the knee.

1 Put a tick beside the sentences that are true and a cross beside the sentences that are false.

☐ **a** The 21st century has much more technology than the 19th century had.

☐ **b** The term 'junk food' would not have been around in the 19th century.

☐ **c** Some children did not have to go to school in the 19th century.

☐ **d** Love of music in New Zealand developed only in the late 20th century.

☐ **e** Some children rode horses to school in the 19th century.

☐ **f** 19th century children were already learning to be 'couch potatoes'.

Richard Pearse's flying machine

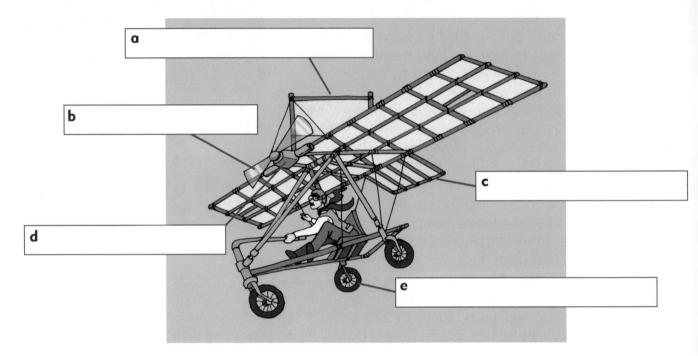

a

b

c

d

e

In 1902 Richard Pearse (1877-1953) was a young man in South Canterbury. His father had given him a small farm to work, but Richard's big love was his workshop. He had set it up in an old cottage on the farm.

Richard was an untrained engineer. Locals called him lonely and hermit-like. He was known as 'Mad Pearse'. People said he did not work hard enough on his farm.

Richard is said to have invented many things such as an automatic guitar-playing device, and a bamboo-framed bicycle with four-speed gears and pump-action pedals. He also built things such as a motorised plough, and an automatic potato driller.

He is most famous for taking to the air in powered flight. His fans say he did this on 31 March 1902. That was one year and nine months before Orville Wright flew at Kitty Hawk, North Carolina.

Richard's plane had a two-cylinder engine, a vertical rudder, tricycle undercarriage and propeller forward of the engine. Some people say this plane flew at Waitohi Valley, about 29 km from Timaru. The plane took off from a farm paddock. It climbed slowly and turned right. It flew about 1,200 metres down a riverbed. It then made a forced landing in the water.

Richard rebuilt the plane. He made some changes to it. His fans say that a year later the machine took off past the schoolhouse in the main Waitohi road. It climbed to about three or four metres. It flew about 50 metres before getting stuck in a high gorse hedge.

Other people don't believe it happened like that. They say both flights were in 1903. They say the flights were not controlled. Some even say the flights were made by model aircraft.

But eyewitnesses said he flew. Parts of the plane have been found.

Nobody knows for sure because Richard did not keep good records. It seems that he himself did not really think he could call his efforts true flight. He did claim to have invented ailerons. They are the flaps on the rear edge of plane wings that give control.

1 Write the five main features of Richard's plane in the boxes on the drawing.

The 1905 rugby tour

Rugby got its name from Rugby School in England. One day schoolboys were playing a scrummaging game with a ball. A boy grabbed the ball and ran with it. The game of rugby was born.

Men played rugby in three-quarter-sleeved jerseys, knickerbockers and stockings. Refs wore suits, high collars and walking boots without sprigs.

In 1905 a New Zealand rugby team toured Britain. To start with, newspapers called the team 'Maorilanders' or 'Fernlanders' but by the end of

THE MOA AND THE LION.

the tour newspapers were calling them the All Blacks. The name may have come from the colour of the team's all-black playing gear. Or it may have come from when the 'l' was dropped in by mistake when a journalist referred to the team as being so fast that they were 'all backs'.

The first All Blacks are known as the 'Originals'. They played 35 matches and won 34. They lost the test match against Wales, 3-0. New Zealand centre three-quarter Robert Deans insisted he scored a try against the Welsh. Ace All Black goalkicker Billy Wallace would have had an easy conversion. Robert claimed the Welsh players shifted the ball back after he scored. The referee was a long way behind and didn't see it.

Newspapers raved about the team. They said the team was a blaze of glory. They said the players went into Britain like lambs but left like lions. The High Commissioner in London cabled the scores to Richard Seddon, the New Zealand Premier. The Premier kept interrupting Parliament to announce the scores. He thought a photo of the team should be hung in every school in New Zealand.

The team got a public reception in Auckland. Shops were closed. Factory work stopped. Offices were empty. Captain David Gallaher talked to the crowd, saying he had only one bit of advice for another team and that was to play the Welsh matches first. David Gallaher later fought in World War 1. He died of wounds he got at Passchendaele. When the All Blacks went back to play Wales in 1924 they won 19 points to 0.

1 Check out the cartoon and write answers to the following.

a year drawn _____

b country Moa stands for _____

c points that country scored _____

d country lion stands for _____

e points that country scored _____

f type of ball on ground _____

g country feeling on top _____

h country feeling helpless _____

World War 1

New Zealand troops at Passchendaele.

On 4 August 1914, the Prime Minister announced that New Zealand was at war. It was going to help Britain fight its enemy, Germany.

On 25 April 1915, Australian and New Zealand Army Corps (Anzacs) landed at a cove on Gallipoli in Turkey. It later became known as Anzac Cove. The Anzacs were there to fight the Turks. Turkey was on the side of Germany. The Turks were guarding the steep sides of the Dardanelles. This was a narrow strait of water which connected the Black Sea with the Mediterranean. Many Anzacs were killed during the landing. Survivors had to fight heat, dust, mud, rats, too little food and water, lice, dysentery and flies as well as the Turks. In May there was an eight-hour stop in the fighting. This was to let both sides bury the rotting dead.

Some 2,700 New Zealanders died at Gallipoli and 4,700 were wounded. In December 1915 the troops were taken off Gallipoli. They had not won but New Zealand soldiers had made a name for themselves. They were heroes. New Zealand thanks and remembers all its soldiers on Anzac Day.

The New Zealand Army joined in the fight against the Germans in France and Belgium. Nearly 50,000 New Zealanders were killed or wounded. Anzacs also fought at Passchendaele. There was so much mud that tanks sometimes sank almost out of sight.

At the start of the war there were enough New Zealand volunteers. But in 1916 the government had to start conscription. This means calling men up to join the forces. The public was angry at men who didn't want to fight. Often the army dragged these men to the front anyway as a punishment.

A battalion of Maori went overseas to fight. Waikato and Taranaki tribes refused to get involved in the war. Maori were not conscripted until 1918. Waikato tribes refused to be conscripted.

People in New Zealand did not like Germans at this time. Some firms with German names changed their names. Some who didn't were attacked. A German butcher got anonymous letters and telegrams. People threw bricks through his shop window. A university professor of modern languages was sacked because he was German. Even the word 'kindergarten' was disliked because it was a German word.

In November 1918 the war ended. Germany was beaten. People rushed into streets. They cheered, sang and waved flags. They hugged each other or shook hands.

New Zealand troops in France.

9780170217804

1 Write down the names of the following places on the map.

a the sea
d the country

b the peninsula
e the big sea joined to the other sea by the strait

c the strait
f the cove where the Anzacs landed

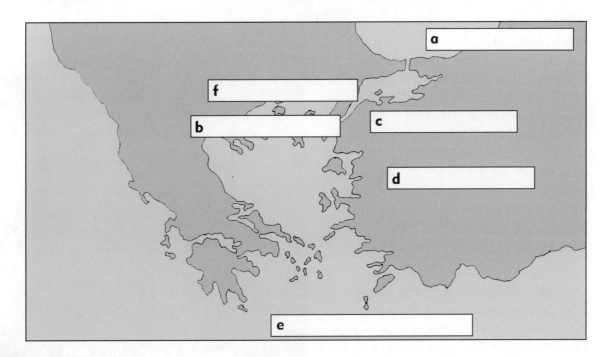

a

f

b

c

d

e

2 Write down the years that the following took place.

a World War 1 started _____

b World War 1 ended _____

c The Anzacs fought at Gallipoli _____

d The New Zealand government brought in conscription _____

3 Write down the names of two countries who were:

a friends of New Zealand during World War 1 _____

_____

b enemies of New Zealand during World War 1 _____

_____

4 Look at the magazine illustration. Write down answers to the following.

a What date? _____

b Which war? _____

c Name for roll of wounded or dead soldiers? _____

d What kind of list? _____

NEW ZEALAND'S
ROLL OF HONOUR
1915

THE AUCKLAND WEEKLY NEWS
ILLUSTRATED LIST

World War 1 killed about nine million people in the world. The great flu epidemic that raged around the world in 1918 killed about 21 million. Flu is short for influenza. The estimated deaths for New Zealand were between six and nine thousand people. The flu was known as the Black Flu because people sometimes turned black after dying. An epidemic is a disease that happens in a place for a short time and affects many people there.

In October 1918 the SS *Niagara* arrived in Auckland with the Prime Minister and Minister of Finance. They had been to a war-time conference in Europe. There were many cases of flu on board. A crew member had died. People later blamed the ship for bringing the flu. But flu cases had been reported earlier.

Trying to keep the flu bugs away – Christchurch 1918.

When war ended in November record crowds took to the streets. They came in contact with the deadly flu.

The Health Department gave sick people small bottles of stout, whisky and brandy. That eased pain for a bit but did not cure the flu. Special spray chambers were set up. They treated up to 30 people at a time. People lined up and got sprayed with a zinc-sulphate solution. It was supposed to kill the bugs but it didn't. Other methods were tried such as spraying mail with formalin to stop letter-readers getting the flu.

Emergency kitchens were set up. They were for families where nobody was well enough to make meals. Many volunteers worked without thinking of their own safety. A lot of doctors were still overseas because of the war. Private cars were used as ambulances. In Auckland dead bodies were kept in Victoria Park before burial, special funeral trains took them and mourners to the cemetery.

Towns became ghost towns. Trams stopped running. Many theatres, cinemas, pubs, schools, shops, churches closed. Race meetings were cancelled. Coal supplies from mines ran down. Children looked after sick relatives. One job was to put a white flag on the mail box as a sign that a dead body needed collecting.

Workers were shocked at the awful living conditions of some people. Too many people knew nothing about how to keep clean and how infection spread. The flu led to more health inspectors being appointed. There were also more school nurses to teach children how to stay clean.

9780170217804

1 ▷ The following are some things that happened during the flu epidemic. They are CAUSES because they caused a RESULT to happen. For each CAUSE, write one RESULT.

a The SS *Niagara* had sick people on it. _____

b War ended in November. _____

c Workers were shocked at living conditions. _____

d Many children did not know how to stay clean. _____

e White flags were put on mail boxes. _____

f Sick people were given alcohol to drink. _____

g Spray chambers sprayed people. _____

h There were not enough ambulances to cope. _____

i Many doctors were still overseas. _____

j People stopped going to town. _____

2 ▷ Write the number of each paragraph in the box at the beginning of the paragraph. Finish the following by writing numbers in the gaps.

a Specific months are mentioned in paragraphs _____ and _____.

b The meanings of influenza and epidemic are in paragraph _____.

c Efforts to teach people about hygiene are mentioned in paragraph _____.

d The effect on entertainment is mentioned in paragraph _____.

e Special inhalation chambers are mentioned in paragraph _____.

3 ▷ Check out the picture and write answers to fill the following gaps.

a This picture was taken in Christchurch in the year _____.

b The word for which 'flu' is the short version is _____.

c The abbreviation for 'Government' is _____.

d The 'medicines' are the three alcoholic drinks called

_____,

_____, and

_____.

Two famous dolphins

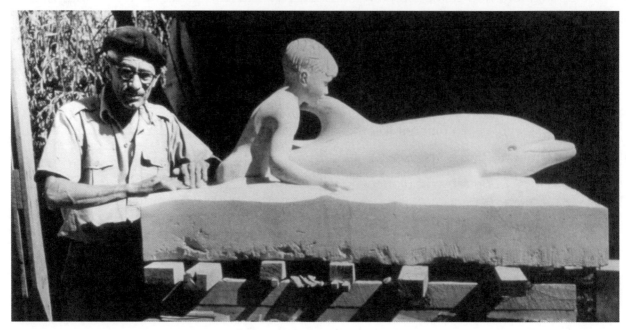

Sculptor Russell Clark putting the finishing touches to his sculpture of Opo.

One day in the late 1880s a steamer was doing the run between Wellington and Nelson. People on board saw a dolphin racing alongside. From then until 1912 this dolphin met almost every steamer on the run. Day and night. He was given the name Pelorus Jack after the place he swam in – Pelorus Sound.

When Pelorus Jack leapt half out of the water, it was said he glowed like a ball of fire. Water sparks streamed from his body. He swam beside steamers and raced about bows. He liked to swim up to the hull and rub his back along the iron plates. People said his eyes looked almost human.

Pelorus Jack became known throughout the world. Overseas visitors to New Zealand made the return trip from Wellington to Nelson especially to see him.

Once someone on board a steamer fired at Pelorus Jack with a rifle. People demanded a law be passed to protect the dolphin and in 1904 the law was passed.

Suddenly in April 1912 he disappeared. Never again was Pelorus Jack seen. Nobody knew what had happened to him. Some people thought he had been shot.

In 1955 fishermen in Hokianga saw a female bottlenose dolphin swimming beside their boats. She even liked them to scratch her with an oar. In the Christmas holidays hundreds of people crowded the beaches at Opononi. The dolphin, now called Opo, came almost every day to play.

Opo seemed to recognise some children. She let them stroke and scratch her. She played with a ball. She even gave some small children short rides on her back.

Opo became world famous. Millions saw her on TV in America and Canada.

The government decided to give her special protection. At midnight on 8 March 1956 a special protection act was passed. Opo hadn't appeared that day. Next day she was found dead. She was jammed among rocks. Some people said she had been stunned by explosives.

Opo was buried onshore. All business in Opononi closed for the day. The New Zealand flag was flown at half-mast.

9780170217804

1 Fill out the chart to show ways Pelorus Jack and Opo were the same and ways they were different.

		Pelorus Jack	Opo
a	type of animal		
b	how they got their name		
c	time they were famous		
d	place they got famous		
e	depth of ocean they played in		
f	relationship with people		
g	popularity		
h	protection		
i	when they died		
j	how they died		

2 Write on the map the names of the following places and islands to do with the two dolphins.

a one of the 3 main islands of New Zealand

b one of the 3 main islands of New Zealand

c the city

d the Sound

e the city

f the small town

g the harbour

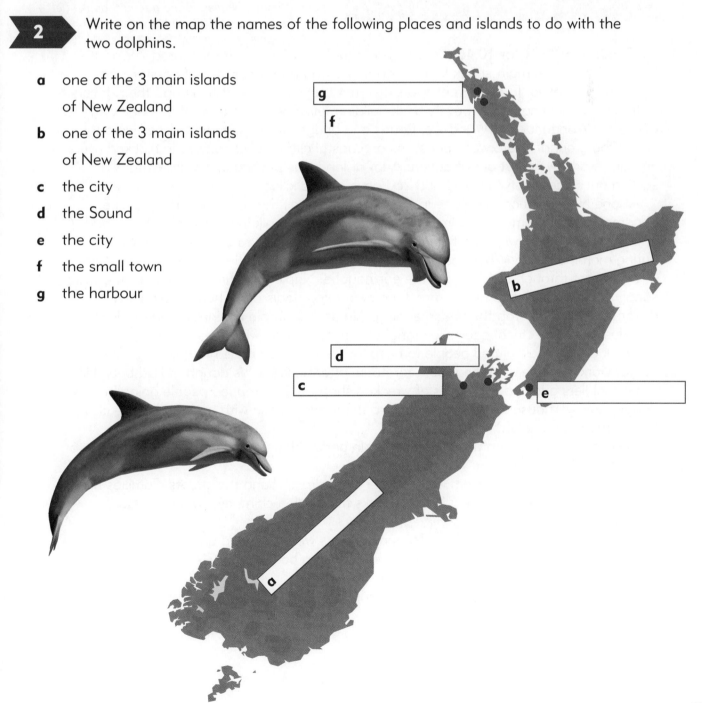

Napier earthquake of 1931

Nurses' home, Napier before the earthquake (left), after the earthquake (above).

On 3 February 1931, at 10.46 a.m., an earthquake hit Napier. It measured 7.9 on the Richter Scale. The main shock lasted about two and a half minutes. Two-storeyed buildings collapsed. In one street two sides met burying a row of taxis and their drivers.

In nearby Hastings almost every brick building fell. There was a lot of damage done to Gisborne, Wanganui and Woodville. Roads and bridges were destroyed. Trees were torn out of the ground. There were landslides on coastal cliffs. Lakes formed in blocked rivers. Freezing works were put out of action. A lot of land was pushed upwards. Water was sucked out to sea. Between 250 and 260 people were killed.

At one Napier school everyone in the playground was thrown to the ground. The headmaster told them to go home. He said they should walk in the middle of the road. At another school a girl who had been naughty had been made to stay in the classroom during morning break. When the quake hit, a teacher ran back inside and rescued her.

Fire swept through Napier after the earthquake. Napier had fire engines but the water supply was wrecked. Firemen pumped the swimming pools dry. Then buildings were dynamited to try to stop the fire spreading. Almost the whole business area of Napier was destroyed. Electrical cables lay tangled with telephone wires.

Truck drivers took injured people to hospital. Tents were pitched for patients. One doctor worked in the operating room for hours after he knew his daughter had been killed.

Old soldiers guarded the goods of wrecked shops. They stopped people going into danger areas. Thousands of people took to the roads. Those with undamaged houses locked them up and left.

Camps for homeless families were set up in parks. Notices were pasted everywhere to tell people what to do.

Clean water was drawn from wells. Water carts drove round the streets. Families filled buckets and kerosene tins. People used bricks from fallen chimneys to make places outside to cook in.

There were many aftershocks. 674 small quakes were recorded until the end of May. A fortnight after the earthquake men were working on a beach near Gisborne. Suddenly a large bank of boulders rose out of the sea.

Laws made it compulsory to make new buildings earthquake-proof. Napier was rebuilt.

9780170217804

Answers

How much do you know already? – page 4
A 1 Waitangi | 2 Russell
3 Opononi | 4 Waitemata
5 Auckland | 6 White Island
7 Tauranga | 8 Ngaruawahia
9 Young Nick's Head | 10 Mt Tarawera
11 Pink and White Terraces | 12 Mt Taranaki
13 Tongariro | 14 Napier
15 Golden Bay | 16 Wellington
17 Cook Strait | 18 Hokitika
19 Timaru | 20 Dunedin
B 1 a 2 b 3 b 4 c 5 c 6 a
7 b 8 c 9 b 10 a 11 b 12 a
13 c 14 c 15 a 16 b 17 c 18 b
19 b 20 a

First arrivals – page 6
ACROSS: 1 land, 2 colder, 5 tangatawhenua,
6 meet, 9 radiocarbon, 12 Kupe, 13 Maori,
15 south, 16 Hawaii
DOWN: 1 legend, 2 canoe, 3 date, 4 Tahiti, 5 tamariki,
7 tribe, 8 Hawaiki, 10 birds, 11 write, 14 few

Tasman saw New Zealand in 1642 – page 7
1 a New Zealand
b the Netherlands or Holland
c Dutch d 56
e Staten Landt, Zeelandia Nova, Nieuw Zealand,
New Zealand
2 any order – Tasman Bay, Tasman Mountains,
Abel Tasman National Park, Tasman Glacier,
Tasman Valley, Mt Tasman

Captain Cook arrived in 1769 – page 8
1 a New Zealand b Pacific Ocean
c Australia d Indian ocean
e Cape of Good Hope f Africa
g South America h Atlantic Ocean
i Europe j England
2 a Cook's Beach b Cook's Gardens
c Cook Rock d Cook Strait
e Mount Cook National Park
f Mount Cook g Cook Stream

Early visitors – page 10
1 a whale b missionary c sealer d trader
2 Green: Maori carvings, kumara, shrunken Maori
heads, fresh pork, Maori mats, flax, fresh water,
kauri timber, Maori spears. Blue: muskets, nails,
axes, tomahawks, blankets, alcohol, spades.

The Treaty of Waitangi – page 11
1 a of Waitangi b William Hobson
c He iwi tahi tatou; We are one people,
d Maori chiefs e Union Jack
f cloaks, flax skirts (Heke, shaking hands with
Hobson, has a pakeha cap on)
g formal clothes: missionary black, naval uniforms
2 James Busby from Britain, William Hobson of the
British Royal Navy, the ship William came to NZ
on, James Busby's house at Waitangi, Maori for
'We are one people', a treaty is an agreement.

The arrival of European settlers – page 12
1 red = Europe brown = Britain
green = New Zealand yellow = Africa
blue = Atlantic, Southern, Pacific
2 a true b true c false
d true e true f false
g false h false

Hone Heke and the flagpole – page 13
1 Any of the following: it was taking away the mana of
the chiefs, NZ was becoming too British, the chiefs
were equal with the British Queen so their flag should
be flying alongside, the British settlers were buying
too much land from the tribes, the government and
capital had been sifted to Auckland, this took trade
away from the Bay of Islands, the flagpole had
neither blood nor bones so it would not feel pain.
2 Treaty of Waitangi, first flagpole put up, Maori
cut down flagpole, Kororareka wrecked, War in
North, Peace in North, Kawiti's son organises new
flagpole.

The first Maori king – page 15
1 a Law of God and the Queen
b Pakeha Governor
c Maori King OR b Maori King
d Pakeha Governor
2 Family was connected to the leaders of the main
ancestral canoes, was a great warrior, father was
a famous tohunga, tribal area had the mighty
Waikato river and the famous Taupiri Mountain,
was a central place for other tribes to visit, had
kai moana and food from rivers, land and bush
3 a 1858 b Tawhiao
c 1894 d King
e Koroki f Queen: Te Atairangikaahu

The 19th century land wars – page 16
1 a Pakeha b Pakeha c Maori
d Pakeha e Maori f government
g Maori h Maori i government
j Maori k government l government
m Maori
2 a i Waikato, ii Taranaki, iii Bay of Plenty,
iv East Coast

Gold rushes in the 1860s – page 18
1 a dangerous b industries
c Arrowtown d Shantytown
2 a Colville, Kuaotunu, Whitianga, Pauanui,
Whangamata, Golden Cross, Waihi, Paeroa,
Thomas, Coromandel
b a Waihi b 45

The story of Parihaka – page 20
1 e, b, d, a, f, c
2 a confiscated b bullocks and horses
c dog d Taranaki,
e New Plymouth f Parihaka
g two or three

Taming of forest – page 22
1 a fireplace b oiled calico

c fern   d dirt
e axe   f jobs and responsibilities
g post and rail   h creek
i walking, heifer, horse   j home first aid
k flour bag clothes l grass broom
2 a fireplace   b fern   c oiled calico
d timber   e dirt   f kitchen
g bedroom   h berries   i eels
j pig, pork   k creek   l water
m fernroot

Refrigeration – page 24
ACROSS: 1 export, 3 chambers, 6 freezingworks,
10 London, 12 Dunedin, 13 meat, 14 sailing ship,
16 frozen, 17 tropics.
DOWN: 2 trip, 4 market, 5 sparks, 7 refrigeration,
8 England, 9 Smithfield, 11 butter, 15 sheep.

Tarawera and White Island – page 25
1 TARAWERA – year of eruption: 1886, number
killed: over 100, Damage to property: destroyed
whole villages.
WHITE ISLAND – year of eruption: 1914, number
killed: 10, Damage to property: destroyed camp
and sulphur plant.
2 a White   b Whakaari   c Wakatane
d Tarawera   e Te Wairoa   f Pink and White
g Te Ariki

Women were allowed to vote – page 26
1 S (Sheppard), U (suffrage), F (franchise), F
(unfeminine), R (dry), A (Australia), G (Wyoming), E
(women), T (Parliament), T (politics), E (New Zealand).
2 a Suffragette
b a woman who works to get the vote for women

Old age pensions – page 27
a x   b x   c x   d x
e x   f ✓   g ✓

The Boer War of 1899-1902 – page 28
1 a F   b O   c F   d O   e O
2 a wounded   b died of disease
c killed in action   d killed in accidents

Life in the 19th century – page 29
a ✓   b ✓   c ✓
d x   e ✓   f x

Richard Pearse's flying machine – page 30
1 a vertical rudder   b propeller
c ailerons   d two cylinder engine
e tricycle undercarriage

The 1905 rugby tour – page 31
a 1905   b NZ   c 829
d England   e 39   f rugby football
g NZ   h England

World War 1 – page 32
1 a Black Sea   b Gallipoli Peninsula,
c Dardanelles Strait   d Turkey
e Mediterranean Sea   f Anzac Cove
2 a 1914   b 1918
c 1915   d 1916
3 a Australia, Britain   b Germany, Turkey
4 a 1915   b World War I
c Roll of Honour   d illustrated

The terrible flu epidemic of 1918 – page 34
1 a People blamed it for bringing the flu.
b Record crowds took to the street.
c More health inspectors were appointed.
d More school nurses were appointed.
e Workers come to collect dead bodies.
f People felt better for a bit but not cured.
g Did not kill bugs.
h Private cars used.
i Volunteers worked.
j Towns become ghost towns.
2 a 2 and 3   b 1   c 7
d 6   e 4
3 a 1918   b influenza
c government   d stout, whisky, brandy

Two famous dolphins – page 36
1 a PJ = male dolphin; Opo = female dolphin
b PJ named after Pelorus Sound; Opo named
after Opononi,
c PJ 1880s-1912; Opo 1955-56
d PJ from Wellington to Nelson; Opo at Opononi
e PJ in deep channels; Opo in shallow water
f PJ with people on big boats; Opo with people
in water
g PJ world-famous; Opo world-famous;
h PJ special protection; Opo special protection,
I PJ in 1912; Opo in 1956,
j PJ just disappeared; Opo jammed among rocks
2 a South   b North   c Nelson
d Pelorus   e Wellington   f Opononi
g Hokianga

Napier earthquake of 1931 – page 38
1 1931, February, 3rd 10.46 am, Napier (Hawke's
Bay), 7.9, 2 and a half minutes, 250-260, 674
recorded until end of May
2 a to measure size of earthquake
b to blow up buildings to stop fires
c to get water to fight fire
d to take injured to hospital
e as guards
f to collect clean water from carts
g to build outdoor fireplaces
h to house homeless
3 clockwise: Gisborne, Hastings, Woodville, Wanganui
4 a Nurses' home   c 3   e pole at right

The Great Depression of the 1930s – page 40
a unemployment   b Statistics New Zealand
c number of unemployed   d thousands
e 5   f census
g no   h 1936
i 55 thousand   j gone down
k 1916   l 1926
m more

Ernest Rutherford, a Kiwi genius – page 41
a Ernest   b Nelson
c Nobel Prize   d chemistry
e atom   f Cambridge
g nuclear   h golf and motoring
i Westminster   j Albert Einstein

Jack Lovelock's gold medal – page 42
1 a 12   b 18   c 26   d 39
2 a Yvette Williams   b Murray Halberg,
c Peter Snell (or vice-versa)   d John Walker

9780170217804

e   Mark Todd   f   Mark Todd
g   Barbara Kendall   h   Danyon Loader
i   Rob Waddell
j   Sarah Ulmer, Georgina & Caroline Evers-Swindell
k and l Valerie Vili, Georgina & Caroline Evers-Swindell

'Our Jean' was a famous flyer – page 43
1 a New Zealand   b Tasman
c England   d South Atlantic
e India   f Brazil

World War 2 – page 44
1 Italy, Germany, Japan
2 a Hiroshima and Nagasaki b Winston Churchill
c Charles Upham   d Michael Savage
e Cobber Kain   f Te Moananui-a-Kiwa Ngarimu
g Pearl Harbour   h Italy
i Bernard Freyberg j VE Day
3 a entering   b Japan
c in case of attack and they were killed or wounded
d to plug up their ears and bite down on during an attack

Edmund Hillary and Mt Everest – page 46
1 B (Buckingham), E (New Zealand), E (Nepal), K (Drake), E (dehydration), E (ice-ace), P (Sherpa), E (Elizabeth), R (Britain) Answer = beekeeper.
2 a 9   b Nepal   c Everest
d Hillary   e 1953

The Auckland Harbour Bridge – page 48
1 a Waitemata   b Northcote   c Erin
2 a reinforced   b bedrock
c cantilever   d truss

Entertainment – page 49
1 only the Vietnam War gets a tick
2 a 52 m in Wellington at Exhibition, b at Exhibition eg. dodgems, c booming laugh, d famous band visited NZ, e radio star, f quiz show, g *It's in the Bag*, h radio star

The move from imperial to metric – page 50
1 (any order) Calculations can be done more easily using decimals, almost all other countries in the world had metric and metric was easier for trade.
2 a 20   b 10   c 12   d 50

The *Wahine* disaster – page 51
a north   b about 6.30 am   c Barrett Reef
d no   e 10.15   f broke
g noon   h 12.15   i 1.10
j because of the lean (list) of the ship
k 200   l a mile   m no
n between Camp Bay and Hind's Point
o Seatoun   p East

The great Maori land march – page 52

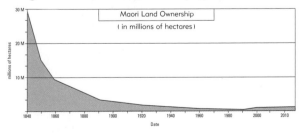

Maori Land Ownership
(in millions of hectares)

The Bastion Point protest – page 53
1840 = Crown pressed to buy land to build Auckland;
1887 = Government took Bastion Point for a fort;
1950s Crown evicted Maori from Orakei Marae;
1976 = Crown refused to return land; 1977 = Maori occupied Bastion Point; 1978 = Government sent to police and Army to get rid of protesters;
1990s = Crown returned some land

The Mt Erebus plane crash – page 54
1 a South   b Erebus   c McMurdo
d McMurdo   e Scott   f Ross
2 a 257   b 3,794 metres
c tomb   d crevasses

The Springbok tour of 1981 – page 55
a Springbok rugby   b South Africa
c separation of races d no
e rugby   f Halt All Racists Tours
g against   h for
i left   j helmets and wooden shields
k shouting and throwing things at each other and the policeman
l long batons

The Waitangi Tribunal – page 56
a Maori   b Waitangi Tribunal
c Maori   d Waitangi Tribunal
e Maori   f Waitangi Tribunal
g Maori   h Waitangi Tribunal
i Maori (also Pakeha and Waitangi Tribunal)
j Maori, Pakeha   k Pakeha
l Maori   m Maori
n Waitangi Tribunal   o Maori, Pakeha
p Pakeha

Kiwi hero Sir Peter Blake – page 57
a New Zealand   b England   c Antarctic
d Brazil   e Amazon

The sinking of the *Rainbow Warrior* in 1985 – page 58
a 1985   b Bromhead   c arrogance
d potential   e New Zealand f France
g France   h *Rainbow Warrior*
i Greenpeace   j one   k Auckland
l limpet mines   m Operation Satanic

New Zealand's first America's Cup win in 1995 – page 59
a 1848 Garrands made the Cup
b 1851 The Old Mug was first raced for
c 1983 The Louis Vuitton Cup was first raced for
d 1995 NZ won the Cup for the first time
e Garrards mended the Cup

The Helen Years – page 60
1 a Wellington   b Parliament, Beehive
c Prime Minister   d 9   e Labour
2 PM; 1st elected female PM of NZ; in Top 20 World's Most Powerful Women; won UN Environment Programme Champions of the Earth; Minister for Arts, Culture and Heritage; involved in the NZ Security Intelligence Service; patron of NZ Rugby League; Administrator of the United Nations Development Programme; 1st female to lead it

New Zealand becomes Middle Earth – page 60
1 a Ngauruhoe   b Mt Doom   c Frodo

2 Filmed by Kiwi director Peter Jackson
3 Got NZ many fans, many tourists visited/visit to see movies places, overseas people learned where NZ was in world, presented marketing opportunity as name has stuck.

New Zealand's first VC – page 62
1 a rough, unsealed   b mountainous, isolated
   c fighting terrorism   d NZ's SAS
   e saved fellow soldier by carrying him through enemy and friendly fire
3 Went to home-coming in Te Kaha, gave all his medals to nation

All Whites make history – page 63
1 a NZ   b Italy   c South Africa
   d France   e Bahrain   f Slovakia
   g Australia
2 a teams qualified
   b NZ's Cup ranking at end of Cup
   c NZ World ranking at beginning of Cup
   d NZ's World ranking at end of Cup

New Zealand's first Super City – page 64
1 a Auckland   b harbour, sea
   c Sky City Tower   d 2010
   e 8   f eco, most liveable
2 First super city, contributes 35% of NZ GDP, 1 of just few world cities that produced more than 30% of country's GDP, well over 1m people

Pike River – page 65
1 a coal
   b Brunner, Dobson, Strongman, Pike River
   c explosion, gas poisoning
2 Brunner, Huntly 1914, Kaitangata, Pike River, Strongman, Huntly 1939, Dobson

Christchurch earthquake – page 66
1 a state of emergency   b evacuated
   c adjourned   d traumatised
   e infrastructure   f liquefaction
2 a Yes   b 12.51 pm 22 Feb 2011
   c No
   d Buildings in the photo are residential and away from the city centre where the mulit-storey buildings were located.

New Zealand 100% Pure – page 68
1 a and b clean, green, spectacular, paradise
2 a 100% Pure
   b NZ Youngest country on Earth
   c 100% Pure You
3 a launching of 100% Pure NZ brand
   b 2007 advertising campaign
   c TV commercial made with Tourism NZ
   d featured in the TV commercial
   e brand aimed at German tourists
   f NZ 100% revives you
   g NZ never leaves you
   h NZ, it's about time
   i NZ has the holiday for you
4 In comparison to other countries it is and it is working hard to fix problems.

Just a few reasons why New Zealand is special – page 70
In order from top to bottom:
1887, birth of Katherine Mansfield, 1893, first car imported, 1901, main trunk railway opened, 1915, 1985, Keri Hulme's Booker Prize, 1987, High-Tech Games, 1993, 1999, American Presidents' visit, 1999, 2011

Final challenge – page 72

1 land
2 Kupe
3 home/land
4 canoes
5 17th
6 Holland/Netherlands
7 Holland/Netherlands
8 Britain/England
9 scurvy
10 *Endeavour*
11 1840
12 William Hobson
13 chiefs
14 We are one people
15 English, Maori
16 true
17 months
18 Hone Heke
19 4
20 engineering
21 Waikato
22 priest/expert
23 Queen
24 tribes
25 North
26 saps
27 land
28 Waihi
29 gold
30 forest/bush
31 Tarawera
32 Whiti
33 Taranaki
34 albatross
35 Dunedin
36 South Africa
37 Holland/Netherlands
38 Riders
39 slates
40 catapult
41 vote
42 New Zealand
43 government
44 Old Age
45 All Blacks
46 Gallipoli
47 conscription
48 flu
49 depression
50 pilots/fliers
51 Earnest Rutherford
52 Westminster
53 Berlin
54 Adolf Hitler
55 Jack Lovelock
56 Wellington
57 1939
58 Britain
59 Prime Minister
60 yes
61 USA
62 Victoria Cross
63 Japan
64 Himalayas
65 Edmund Hillary
66 Queen Elizabeth
67 Bag
68 decimal currency/metric
69 television
70 Auckland
71 march/step
72 Wellington/Parliament
73 red socks
74 Bastion
75 fire
76 Mother
77 South
78 Scott
79 Springbok
80 apartheid
81 Atlas
82 Waitangi
83 holiday
84 two
85 Greenpeace
86 France
87 Russell Coutts
88 Australia
89 King Dick
90 Short stories
91 Peter Jackson
92 tennis
93 Park
94 car
95 Nelson
96 USA
97 Swimming
98 Maori activist
99 East Timor
100 terrorism

Bonus points – page 72
a Abel Tasman   b Jack Lovelock   c Captain Cook   d Edmund Hillary
e Kate Sheppard   f Willie Apiata   g Peter Blake   h Ernest Rutherford

1 Fill out this data file on the Napier earthquake.

Napier Earthquake Data File

Year: _____

Month: _____

Day: _____

Time: _____

Place: _____

Size of quake: _____

Length of main shock: _____

Deaths: _____

Aftershocks: _____

---

2 Write down one thing that each of the following was used for in the quake.

a Richter Scale _____

b dynamite _____

c swimming baths _____

d trucks _____

e old soldiers _____

f kerosene tins _____

g fallen chimneys _____

h camps _____

3 Write in the missing place names on the map by using the following information.

a Wanganui is west of Napier.

b Gisborne is north-east of Napier.

c Hastings is south of Napier.

d Woodville is south-west of Napier.

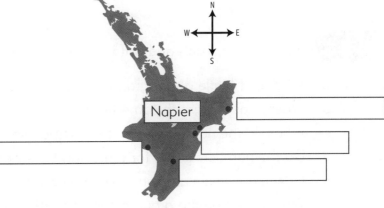

4 Fill in the gaps to finish the following report on the photographs on page 36.

---

a) Name of building: _____

b) Size of building: *one of the largest in Napier*

c) Number of storeys: _____

d) Number of dead: *8*

e) Object still standing after the quake: _____

26 The Great Depression of the 1930s

UNEMPLOYMENT

A depression is a drop in business activity. It causes people to lose jobs (unemployment). People earn less money. Times get tough.

The Depression of the 1930s was world-wide. New Zealand earned less money for its trade goods so the government looked for ways to save money. Wages and pensions were cut. The school entrance age was raised from five to six. Teachers' colleges closed down. Hospitals were told to reuse old bandages and to cut down on food.

Statistics New Zealand

Unemployment rose. Cheap child labour increased as adult men were laid off. Families were evicted (thrown out) from their houses for not paying rent. People lived in awful houses and huts. They lost furniture because they couldn't keep up payments on it.

Some farmers walked off their land. Swaggers took to the road. Men fled to Australia to look for work. Families split up. People wore patched clothes. Children queued for broken biscuits, rotten fruit and bits of Weet-Bix. Volunteers set up soup kitchens for hungry people.

Some men went to government-run public work camps. They built the Homer Tunnel, planted pine forests, improved parks and school grounds, planted marram grass on sand dunes, dug channels through swamps, cleared trees from rivers, chipped weeds off footpaths, built roads. But some jobs were useless such as digging holes and filling them up again.

Not everybody had a bad time. Some people bartered by swapping goods for services. For example farmers in Taranaki paid a couple of doctors with pigs, hens and potatoes.

There were public protests because the government couldn't fix the depression. People rioted and looted in Auckland, Dunedin, and Wellington.

Good times did not come back to New Zealand until things got better in the United States and Britain. That was in the middle of the 1930s when New Zealand trade began to pick up. Other countries paid better prices for New Zealand's goods. People cheered up.

> **1** Look at the graph and write answers to these questions.

a What is the title of the graph? _____

b Where has the graph come from? _____

c What do the numbers down the left side show? _____

d Do the numbers stand for tens, hundreds or thousands? _____

e How many years are shown on the graph? _____

f Which word on the graph means an official count of people? _____

g Are the gaps between the years all the same? _____

h Which year has the highest unemployment? _____

i About how many people were unemployed in that year? _____

j What had happened to unemployment by 1945? _____

k Which year had about the same unemployment as 1945? _____

l Which year had about the same unemployment as 1921? _____

m In 1933 there were about 80,000 unemployed. Is that more OR less than in 1936? _____

9780170217804

Ernest Rutherford, a Kiwi genius

Ernest was born in 1871. His parents farmed near Nelson. At school, Ernest was good at arithmetic and keen on science. He had eleven brothers and sisters. His mother made sure they finished their homework with the saying 'All knowledge is power'.

In his last year Ernest was top of his class in every subject. He was Head Boy, and played in the rugby 1st XV. He won one of ten Junior scholarships for the whole of New Zealand. After he had finished university in New Zealand, he won a science scholarship to Cambridge in England. Later he became a professor in England.

Ernest had great energy and determination. He won many honours, degrees, and medals. In 1908 he won the Nobel Prize for chemistry. He looked after young science students in Britain especially New Zealanders. He was the father of nuclear physics. He changed the way people saw the makeup of the atom. Ernest was Atom Man.

Like two other great scientists, Albert Einstein (1879–1955, German) and Isaac Newton (1642–1727, English), Ernest Rutherford became world-famous. Einstein called Ernest 'a second Newton'.

Ernest invented and experimented. He was willing to find unusual solutions to problems. He said this was because he had been a farmboy in New Zealand. 'We don't have the money,' he said, 'so we have to think.'

His three big discoveries shaped modern science. The first one was that elements can change their structure naturally. The second was the nuclear model of the atom. The third was the splitting of the atom.

In 1934 the *New Zealand Herald* reported that a London crowd saw Ernest, now Lord Rutherford, splitting atoms. People in the Middle Ages who had tried to 'mess around' with elements like this were burned at the stake. Ernest used an apparatus of 100,000 volts to disintegrate atoms at a rate of 1,000 a minute. A wireless system let the audience hear the shells 'bombarding' the atoms.

Ernest liked golf and motoring. He was always proud he was a Kiwi. He died in 1937. His ashes were buried in Westminster Abbey, near Sir Isaac Newton's tomb.

1 Write down the names of the following:

a Rutherford's first name _____

b the place of his early schooling _____

c the prize he won in 1908 _____

d the branch of science for which he won the 1908 prize _____

e what he split _____

f the British university he went to _____

g the physics of which he is 'father' _____

h his two non-work interests _____

i the abbey his ashes are in _____

j the man who called him a second Newton _____

Jack Lovelock's gold medal

Jack was born on the West Coast in 1910. His father died in 1922. In 1928 in Jack's final year at Timaru Boys' High, he won the senior 440 yards, 880 yards and one mile titles. He was school Dux and Head Prefect. He went to Otago University to study medicine. Later he won a scholarship to Oxford University in England. Jack played many sports. But after he broke his leg playing rugby, he spent more time on his running.

At the 1936 Berlin Olympics in Germany, Jack was New Zealand's flag-bearer. Adolf Hitler was leader of Germany and the Nazis. He wanted to use the Olympics to show the world how good the 'pure' German race was.

The big event was the 1,500 metres. Jack was running in it. The start of the race was held up for a few minutes, probably to let Herr Hitler arrive to see the race.

The pistol went off. The runners shot out of their blocks. Jack was small and slim; he had a smooth and easy running style. At 800 m he was third. But he was very fit and could judge races. As the runners came into the back straight for the last time, he made his move. His legs seemed to grow longer. With a burst of speed he swept into the lead. He gave it everything he had. The crowd jumped to its feet. They screamed and cried with excitement. 'Lovelock!' they yelled.

Jack won. He set a new world record of 3 m 47.8 s. This was New Zealand's first Olympic track gold medal. He was crowned with a laurel wreath by a German girl. He was given a small oak tree in a pot. Winners were to plant their oaks in their own country. Jack's oak was planted at Timaru Boys' High School.

Jack went to work in New York. In 1949 he fell onto a railway track in front of an oncoming train and was killed.

Other standout winners of gold medals for New Zealand have been:
Yvette Williams (women's long jump, 1952)
Murray Halberg (5000 m, 1960)
Peter Snell (800 m, 1960)
John Walker (1500 m, 1976)
Mark Todd (horse riding, 1984, 1988)
Barbara Kendall (women's boardsailing, 1992)
Danyon Loader (two swimming golds, 1996)
Rob Waddell (rowing, 2000)
Sarah Ulmer (cycling 2004)
Valerie Vili (shot put 2008)
Georgina & Caroline Evers-Swindell (rowing 2004 & 2008)

1 Write down how old Jack Lovelock was when the following took place.

a Jack's father died _____

b Jack was Dux of his school _____

c Jack won a gold medal _____

d Jack was killed _____

2 Write in each box the name of a New Zealander who won a gold medal in that year.

a 1952	b 1960	c 1960
d 1976	e 1984	f 1988
g 1992	h 1996	i 2000
j 2004	k 2008	l 2008

'Our Jean' was a famous flyer

Jane Gardner Batten (1909–1982), known as Jean, was born in Rotorua. Her mother pinned a newspaper picture of a famous French pilot, who had just flown the English Channel, beside baby Jean's cot.

Her first flight was a joyride with Charles Kingsford Smith in 1929. She shocked her father by saying she wanted to be a flyer. She sold her piano to pay the fares for herself and her mother to go to England two years later. There she learned to fly and got her pilot's licence.

Jean was glamorous and beautiful. Men fell for her. One bought her a de Havilland Gipsy Moth. She decided to break flying records. She was lucky to survive her first efforts. She got caught in a sandstorm over Iraq. When she lost control of the plane, it went into a spin. Her bed that night was under a wing in the desert. Next day she hit another sandstorm and was again forced down. Then the engine failed and she wrecked the plane trying to land. She crawled out unhurt.

Jean had no fear. She was a great navigator. All she had was a watch and compass to help her. She was determined to do well. Bad weather did not put her off. She took big risks. When she flew the Tasman she had no radio or life-saving gear. Before take-off she said that no one was to risk their life looking for her if she went missing.

People called her 'Our Jean'. They said she had beaten the birds at their own game. After she retired, she lived most of her life abroad out of the public eye.

Jean's Solo Records
1933 England to India
1934 England to Australia (new record for women)
1935 Australia to England (first woman to fly both ways)
1935 England to Brazil
1936 England to NZ/Australia to NZ
1937 Australia to England

1 ▶ Write the names of the following in the boxes on the map.

a The country where Jean Batten was born.
b The sea she flew over between Australia and New Zealand.
c The country she left from to fly to Australia in May 1934.
d The sea she flew over between England and Brazil.
e The country to which she flew in 1933 from England.
f The country to which she flew in November 1935 from England.

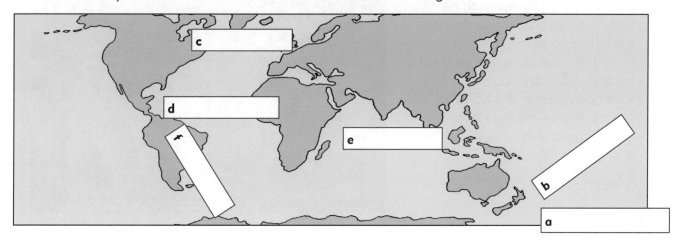

UNIT 30

World War 2

'Cobber' Kain

In 1939 Britain and Germany went to war with each other again. France and Russia came in on the side of Britain. When the Japanese attacked the US naval base of Pearl Harbour in 1941, it brought the US into the war with Britain. Japan and Italy were on Germany's side.

When war started, the New Zealand Prime Minister Michael Savage said 'We range ourselves without fear beside Britain.'

Major-General Bernard Freyberg led the New Zealand Division. Some Kiwis fought in the deserts of North Africa against Germans and Italians. Some fought in the Pacific Islands against Japanese. Some tried to save Greece and Crete from the Germans. Some took part in famous battles such as Monte Cassino in Italy. Many were killed or wounded. Some were captured and put in Japanese and German prisoner of war camps.

'Cobber' Edgar Kain was a Kiwi airman. At 21-years-old, he was the Royal Air Force's crack ace. He wore a tiki. He probably shot down 40 enemy planes before he was killed. Kiwi soldier Charles Upham won the Victoria Cross twice. Te Moananui-a-Kiwa Ngarimu, from the Maori Battalion, also won a VC. Thousands of women joined the women's services. They did not fight, but did many men's jobs. Some worked on farms as land girls.

There was no television so people had to rely on radio and newspapers for news. They listened to speeches by British Prime Minister Winston Churchill.

Japanese planes and submarines prowled close to New Zealand. Many people were scared Japan would attack. Schools practised air-raid drills. Houses had blackouts; they were not allowed to show lights at night. Some Italians and Germans living in New Zealand were locked up on Somes Island in Wellington. Thousands of American soldiers and marines spent time in New Zealand. Many were later killed in the Pacific war.

Some foods were rationed. People were allowed to buy only a certain amount of sugar, butter, cream, tea, meats, and cheese. Other things such as timber, rubber, paper, and petrol were hard to get.

In 1945 Germany surrendered in Europe (VE Day). Japan surrendered after the US dropped atomic bombs on the cities of Hiroshima and Nagasaki (VJ Day). V stood for 'Victory'.

Women in New Zealand digging trenches.

9780170217804

1 Put a cross beside the names of countries that New Zealand fought against in World War 2.

☐ Britain ☐ Russia ☐ USA ☐ Japan

☐ Italy ☐ France ☐ Greece ☐ Germany

2 Write down names for the following.

a Two Japanese cities that had atomic bombs dropped on them.

_____ _____

b The British war-time Prime Minister. _____

c A double VC winner. _____

d The New Zealand Prime Minister who declared war on Germany. _____

e The New Zealand crack ace for the Royal Air Force. _____

f The Maori Battalion soldier who won the VC. _____

g The US naval base that Japan attacked. _____

h The country in which the Battle for Monte Cassino was fought. _____

i The leader of the New Zealand Division in the war. _____

j The day that Germany surrendered. _____

3 Look at the picture below of Devonport (Auckland) students in the 1940s.

a Are the students practising entering OR leaving the air-raid shelter? (Cross one out.)

b Which country did they fear would attack them? _____

c Why did the students wear name tags around their necks? _____

_____

d Why did the students carry tins containing cotton wool and a cork? (Think ears and teeth.) _____

Edmund Hillary and Mt Everest

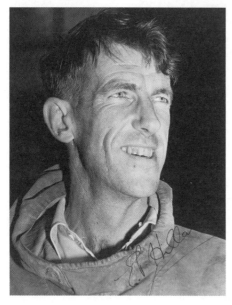

In the 20th century, climbers dreamed of being the first to get to the top of the tallest mountain in the world – Mt Everest. It was in the great mountain range called the Himalayas, on the border between Nepal and Tibet.

Climbers had to plan well. What season was best? Winter has a very cold wind. Summer has a monsoon wind which brings rain and snow. What clothes should they wear? What food and gear should they take? How would their bodies cope with less oxygen?

In 1953 Colonel John Hunt of Britain put together a very strong team of climbers. He included two Kiwis – Edmund Hillary and George Lowe. This was the eighth team to try to reach the top of Everest. There was a lot of planning. The team set up camps. They climbed from the south through Nepal.

Two men in the team tried to get to the top. One of their oxgyen sets did not work properly. They failed.

Next it was the turn of Edmund Hillary and Tenzing Norgay. They were both strong and fit. Edmund Hillary had been born in 1919, in Auckland. Tenzing Norgay was a Sherpa. Sherpas are people who come from the southern slopes of Mt Everest.

Hillary and Norgay waited for dawn. They tried to get warm. To stop dehydration, they had to drink. A small cooker melted ice for water. Hillary's boots were frozen. He tried to thaw them out over the tiny flame. Dressed in their down suits, they put their oxygen sets onto their shoulders and set off.

Several hours later they made it to the top of Everest. Hillary took a photo of Tenzing. Tenzing had the flags of Nepal, the United Nations, India and the Union Jack flying from his ice-axe.

News of the climb was first sent to Buckingham Palace in England. It was the eve of the coronation (crowning) of Queen Elizabeth. The news spread among the crowds lining the coronation route. Thousands of people packed in Piccadilly Circus threw their hats in the air and cheered when they heard.

Newspapers raved about Hillary and Norgay. They compared them to famous heroes from the past such as Drake and Raleigh. The Queen knighted Hillary and Hunt. Norgay got an award. Hillary famously said, 'Well, we knocked the bastard off!'

Statue of Hillary permanently gazing towards Mt Cook/ Aoraki, one of his favourite peaks.

9780170217804

1 Find out the job Edmund Hillary did in New Zealand before his climb up Everest by writing down the answers to the clues in the boxes.

☐ 1st letter of palace that got the news of the climb first.
☐ 2nd (and 5th) letter of country from which Hillary came.
☐ 2nd letter of country Hunt's team climbed through.
☐ 4th letter of past hero that Hillary and Norgay were compared to.
☐ 2nd letter of what Hillary and Norgay tried to stop by drinking.
☐ 3rd (and 6th) letter of where Tenzing had four flags flying from.
☐ 5th letter of people from the southern slopes of Everest.
☐ 1st (and 7th) letter of queen who was crowned in 1953.
☐ 2nd letter of country from which Colonel John Hunt came.

Before he climbed Mt Everest, Edmund Hillary was a _____.

2 Finish the map of the successful climbing route by writing the following information in the correct box.

a The number of camps, including the base camp, set up.
b The country through which the climb was made.
c The name of the highest mountain in the world.
d The name of the Kiwi who reached the summit.
e The year of the climb.

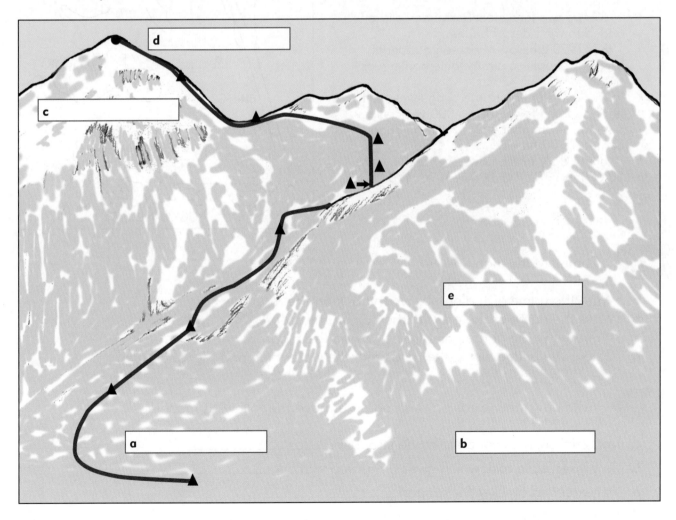

UNIT 32

The Auckland Harbour Bridge

Auckland sits within two harbours. To the west is Manukau Harbour, which flows into the Tasman Sea. On the east is Waitemata Harbour, which opens into the Hauraki Gulf.

BRIDGE DATA FILE

- Spans Waitemata Harbour between Erin Point on south and Northcote Point on north.
- Series of cantilever and suspended spans made of reinforced concrete and steel decks.
- Carried on steel trusses set on six concrete piers on the bedrock.
- Four lanes when first built.
- About 1,030 metres long.
- Cost 7.5 million pounds.
- Took a workforce of 1,000 men 3 1/2 years to build.
- May 1959 a week before bridge officially opened, public allowed to walk over it; St John Ambulance treated many blisters and earaches; a drunk man was the first arrest on bridge.
- 1969 two two-lane steel box girder 'clip-ons' added to the sides of bridge.
- 1987–1990 crossover head-on accidents killed 11 people so a moveable barrier was put in.
- In the last year before the bridge was built, ferries carried fewer than 5,000 vehicles a day; two years after it was built the bridge carried 15,000 a day.
- Average daily traffic flows over bridge were 80,000 in 1970, 140,000 in 1996, 170,000 in 2011.

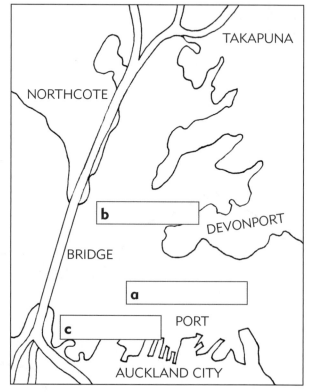

1 Complete the map.

a Write the name of the harbour in the box on the map.
b Write the name of the point in the box on the map.
c Write the name of the point in the box on the map.
d Colour the bridge black, the roads red, the water blue and the land green.

2 Write down the words on this page that have the following meanings.

a material such as concrete made stronger _____
b unbroken solid rock which gives a firm foundation _____
c an extended bracket for support _____
d a rigid framework used for support _____

9780170217804

33 Entertainment

New Zealanders did not get the chance to watch television in their own homes until the 1960s. Until then they had other forms of entertainment such as movie theatres and community sports days.

People loved going to see exhibitions. A big one was the 1939–40 Centennial Exhibition in Wellington. It had a 52-metre-high Centennial Tower which weighed 7,000 tonnes. The aim of the exhibition was to show off New Zealand's progress. But it had fun things too. There was a Playland with a scenic railway and mechanical rides such as 'highland fling' and 'octopus'. There were dodgem cars, a ghost train, and a crazy house. The boom of the Laughing Sailor could be heard all over the grounds.

Election meetings were entertainment. Held in the open-air, they were loud affairs with songs and speeches. People yelled abuse. Often fights broke out.

Music continued to be popular. Musical evenings were held in private houses with recitals and singalongs around the piano. Gramophones had arrived in the 1890s. Overseas opera stars and musicians visited. Even the Beatles came later, in 1964.

Radios arrived in the 1920s. Radio stars had names such as Aunt Daisy and Uncle Scrim. There was a special quiz show featuring children. It was called The Quiz Kids. People listened to rugby matches on the radio. Selwyn Toogood had a radio show called It's in the Bag, which later went on television.

Communities got together to celebrate progress such as the opening of a school or bridge. There might be parades and a half-holiday from school.

During the 1950s experiments in television were made in New Zealand. Regular black and white television broadcasts began in Auckland in 1960, in Christchurch and Wellington in 1961, and Dunedin in 1962. Within a few years more than half the houses had television sets. There was only one channel. Colour arrived in 1973; a second channel in 1975.

1 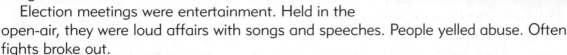 Put a cross or tick in the boxes to show whether New Zealanders would have got television coverage of the following wars in which New Zealand troops fought.

☐ New Zealand Wars (1840s–72)   ☐ World War 2 (1939–45)

☐ Boer War (1899–1902)   ☐ Korean War (1950–1953)

☐ World War 1 (1914–18)   ☐ Vietnam War (1964–1972)

2 Give a few words about each of the following to show who or what they were.

a Centennial Tower _____   **b** Playland _____

c Laughing Sailor _____   **d** Beatles _____

e Aunt Daisy _____   **f** The Quiz Kids _____

g Selwyn Toogood _____   **h** Uncle Scrim _____

The move from imperial to metric

Kiwi money and measurement used to be in the imperial system. Length and area were in inches, feet, yards and miles. Fluid volume was in ounces, pints, gallons. Mass was in ounces, pounds, stones, hundredweights and tons. Money was in pounds, shillings and pence.

This imperial system had been used in Britain for centuries. Early Pakeha settlers brought it out to New Zealand and it stayed for over 150 years.

The symbols used in the imperial system were different to the metric system. For example in 1879 bread cost 7d a 4 lb loaf (sevenpence for a four-pound loaf) and potatoes cost 8s to 11s a cwt (8 to 11 shillings for a hundredweight). Gold miners could pay £1 (one pound) for a few bits of firewood.

The decimal is the basis of the metric system founded by the French several centuries ago. Decimal is a fraction in which the denominator is the power of ten. Denominator is the part of the fraction below the line showing how many equal parts a quantity is divided into, such as the 4 in ¼.

New Zealand decided to bring in decimals because calculations can be done more easily using decimals. Most other countries were using metric so it would make it easier for trade and New Zealand was a big trader.

New Zealand started with the decimalisation of the currency in 1967. DC Day was the 10 July. To start with, some people were very confused. Metrification of weights and measures followed later. There are still people alive who haven't really got into metrics yet.

Old system	New system
pound (quid)	2 dollars
10 shillings	1 dollar
florin (2 shillings)	20 cents
shilling (bob)	10 cents
sixpence (zak, tanner, sprat)	5 cents
threepence (thruppence)	no equivalent
penny (plural was pence)	no equivalent

1 Write down three reasons for New Zealand going metric.

a _____

b _____

c _____

2 Do the following maths and write in the answers.

a How many shillings in a pound?

_____

b How many florins in a pound?

_____

c How many pence in a shilling?

_____

d How many cents would two florins and a shilling make?

_____

9780170217804

The *Wahine* disaster

On the 10 April 1968 the inter-island ferry *Wahine* was on its way from Lyttelton Harbour in Christchurch in the South Island. It had 734 passengers and crew. In Wellington Harbour it was caught in mountainous seas and fierce winds gusting at up to 125 knots. The ferry sank and 51 people died. The official inquiry later found the weather caused the disaster.

Some people were heroes. Two young men risked their lives to save a baby. One took off his own lifejacket and sat the baby on top of it. The men pushed the baby over the waves. A lifeboat paddled for fifteen minutes to reach them.

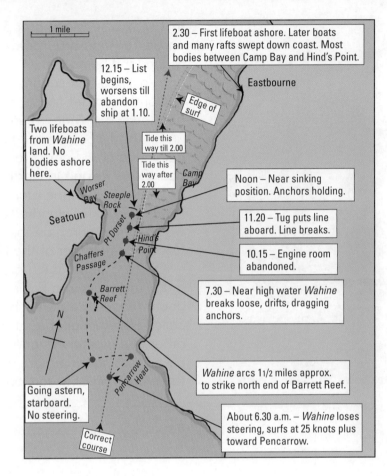

1 Find answers to the following on the map.

a In which direction was the *Wahine* going from Lyttelton? _____

b At what time did the *Wahine* lose its steering? _____

c What 'big black rocks' did the *Wahine* hit? _____

d Did the anchors hold the ship when the crew first put them down? _____

e At what time did the crew give up on the engine room? _____

f What happened to the line that the tug put aboard? _____

g At what time did the anchors start to hold? _____

h At what time did the ship start to lean over? _____

i When did people start to leave the ship? _____

j Why could the crew get only half the number of lifeboats into the water? _____

_____

k At what time did the tide change? _____

l About what distance was it between Pt Dorset and Hind's Point? _____

m Did any bodies wash up on the Seatoun side? _____

n Where did most bodies get washed ashore? _____

o Did the *Wahine* sink opposite Seatoun OR Eastbourne? _____

p Was the mountainous surf on the eastern OR the western side? _____

The great Maori land march

In 1975 some Maori groups got together to make a special group called Te Ropu o te Matakite. This group aimed to stop any more Maori land being lost. It asked 80-year-old Whina Cooper to lead it. She said yes and suggested a land march from the Far North to Parliament to get Maori and Pakeha support. This was called a hikoi, which in Maori means step or march.

On the 14 September 1975 Whina Cooper, holding the hand of her young grand-daughter Irenee, led the marchers from Te Hapua near Cape Reinga in Northland. Thousands of other people joined in on the way down the island. They marched all the way to Wellington. It was 1,120 km. Hundreds of thousands of New Zealanders watched the march on the road or on television. They called Whina Cooper the Mother of the Nation.

On 13 October the marchers were in Wellington. Whina led about 5,000 marchers into Parliament grounds. They gave special papers about Maori land ownership to the Prime Minister. One paper was called a memorial of rights. It came from 200 Maori elders. The other was a petition signed by 60,000 Maori and Pakeha. The papers asked that not one more acre of Maori land be sold. They asked for the protection of Maori land and culture.

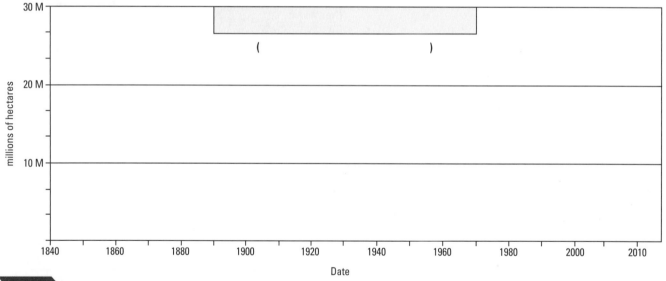

1 Finish the graph on the page by doing the following things.

a Write the title – **Maori Land Ownership** – in the box.
b Write the scale – **in millions of hectares** – in the brackets.
c Put small crosses on the graph to show the following figures:

Date	How much land Maori owned	Date	How much land Maori owned
1840	29.9 m hectares	1920	2.2 m hectares
1852	15.3 m hectares	1939	1.8 m hectares
1860	9.6 m hectares	1975	1.4 m hectares
1891	4.9 m hectares	1986	1.2 m hectares
1911	3.2 m hectares	2011	1.5 m hectares

d Join the crosses in a line.
e Use green to colour in below the line.

9780170217804

37 The Bastion Point protest

Bastion Point is in Auckland. It is near Mission Bay and about 6 km east of Queen Street. Its Maori name is Takaparawha. It used to belong to the Ngati Whatua tribe.

In 1840 the Crown wanted to buy land from Maori to build the new town of Auckland. It put pressure on the chief of Ngati Whatua to sell land. He sold about 1,200 ha to the Crown. Before he died, he got 280 ha kept for the tribe. The Crown (government) kept taking bits of this land. Bastion Point was taken for a fort in 1887. It guarded the entrance to Waitemata Harbour.

Ngati Whatua's papakainga – home patch – was the Orakei Marae on the Okahu Bay foreshore. In the early 1950s Auckland wanted this land for a park. The Crown evicted (asked to leave) Maori from the marae. It made them tenants of state homes nearby. It pulled down their houses and buildings and burned them.

In 1976 the Crown said it was going to put luxury housing on the land. Ngati Whatua demanded the return of the land. The Crown refused. Led by Joe Hawke, a young Ngati Whatua builder, about 150 people occupied Bastion Point in January 1977. They put a few tents and caravans on the site. Several hundred people joined the protest. They put up a meeting house, gateway and watch tower. They planted grass and grew food. Many Maori and Pakeha visited to give support. Drugs and alcohol were not allowed at Bastion Point. Children kept going to school. At 'home' they learned Maori language, custom and history. They learned how to build, clean, and feed large crowds. One teenage protester passed six subjects in School Certificate (a fifth form [Year 11] exam). She said Bastion Point was a turning point in her life. Sad things also happened. A nine-year-old girl died in a fire at the campsite.

The protesters stayed for 506 days. The Courts ruled the protesters were trespassing. In May 1978 the government sent in 600 police backed up by the Army. They arrested over 200 protesters. They destroyed buildings and gardens.

In the early 1990s the Crown gave some land back to Ngati Whatua.

1 In the space after the dates on the following history road, write an event to do with Bastion Point that happened at that time.

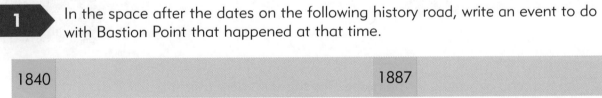

1840		1887

1950s

1976

1977

1978

1990s

The Mt Erebus plane crash

28 November 1979
- An Auckland-based Air New Zealand DC-10 was on a sight-seeing flight over Antarctica's Ross Sea region.
- The slopes of Mt Erebus were covered in ice.
- There were white-out conditions where sky and snow-covered ground seem to join and the pilot's eyes can't tell the difference.

Mt Erebus
- Only active volcano at South Pole.
- 3794 metres high.
- On Ross Island.
- Near McMurdo Sound.
- Near US's McMurdo Station.
- Near New Zealand's Scott Base.

The crash
- The DC-10 crashed into Erebus on the northern side of Ross Island.
- The plane hit the mountain at more than 480 kilometres per hour.
- The 20 crew and 237 passengers were killed.

The crash site
- For hours after the DC-10 fell out of radio contact, flights searched for it.
- The crash site, when found, was called a 'hell-hole'.
- It was steep, snow-covered and had many crevasses.
- Crews had to build a landing pad for US choppers to recover bodies.

Results of crash
- One of world's worst plane disasters.
- Air New Zealand stopped sight-seeing trips to Antarctica.
- Inquiry said airline officials had programmed the plane wrongly.
- Countries with research bases in Antarctica declared crash site a tomb.
- A stainless steel cross is at the edge of crash site.

c) _____ Sound

b) Mt _____

f) _____ ISLAND

d) _____ Station

e) _____ Base

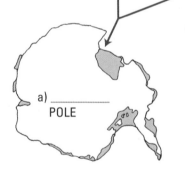

a) _____ POLE

---

1 ▶ Finish the map by writing in the names for the following on it.

a the pole	**b** the mountain	**c** the sound
d the station	**e** the base	**f** the island

2 ▶ Write answers to the following questions.

a How many people were killed in the crash? _____

b How high is Mt Erebus? _____

c What word on this page means 'a place for the dead'? _____

d What word on this page means 'deep holes in snow'? _____

39 The Springbok tour of 1981

In 1981 the South African government had apartheid (separation of races) laws. Blacks did not have equal rights with whites, even thought there were millions more blacks than whites.

Many people around the world thought apartheid was racist. They said South Africa should not be allowed to play sport with other countries until it got rid of apartheid. A Kiwi group was called HART (Halt All Racist Tours).

In July 1981 a rugby team from South Africa came to New Zealand. The players were called Springboks, after an African animal. The tour divided New Zealanders, and even families, into those for the tour and those against it.

Special riot police wore visors and used long batons at anti-tour rallies where protesters wore helmets and carried wooden shields. Many people were arrested. Many were hurt in fights.

Before the first game, in Gisborne, a group of Maori women put broken glass on the field. Police fought protesters throughout the game. Games at Hamilton and Timaru had to be cancelled. In the game against Auckland, a protester dressed as a referee ran on the field at kick-off and stole the ball.

At the final test, in Auckland, about 10,000 protesters were outside the gate. They fought with police. A plane dropped parachute flares and flour bombs on the field. The protesters chanted loudly all through the game.

In the early 1990s South Africa got rid of apartheid.

Atlas

This cartoon shows what New Zealand was like during the 1981 tour. Atlas was a giant in an ancient story who had to stand with the heavens on his shoulders. The police must have felt like Atlas. They were expected to look after everybody's rights including those for the tour and those against it. They were also expected to keep peace between the two sides.

STOP
The '81 Tour
fight apartheid

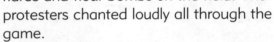

1 Look at the cartoon and answer the following questions.

a Which team was touring New Zealand at this time? _____

b From which country did that team come? _____

c What did apartheid mean? _____

d Does that country still have apartheid? _____

e What sort of ball is the policeman holding? _____

f What does HART stand for? _____

g Are the group on the left for OR against the tour? _____

h Are the group on the right for OR against the tour? _____

i Which group – left OR right – were called protesters? _____

j What did protesters use to protect themselves? _____

k What are the two groups doing? _____

l What 'weapon' did riot police use at this time? _____

The Waitangi Tribunal

Before Pakeha came to New Zealand	After Pakeha came to New Zealand
MAORI	
• owned land as tribes • chiefs had power • tribes governed themselves • was the only culture	• lost land by selling and confiscations • chiefs lost power • had to obey British government • lost out to British culture

• Maori were left with grievances. A grievance is a real or imagined wrong done to a person or a group of people.
• Maori said the Crown/government had broken the Treaty of Waitangi.

• In 1975 the government set up the Waitangi Tribunal to check out Maori grievances. It has Maori and Pakeha members.
• A tribunal is a special court.

1970s Government made Waitangi Day a national holiday.
1980s Government said Maori and Pakeha cultures were equally important. This is called biculturalism.

The Waitangi Tribunal has heard hundreds of cases. Some big ones have involved millions of dollars. They might be about land confiscated by the Crown during the 1860s wars. Or about a factory putting waste into a river or ocean. Or about the government not looking after Te Reo, the Maori language. Or about land taken from Maori in the war to build a runway and instead of being returned after the war, the land was made into a golf course. They may result in the government saying sorry for the Crown's past actions. The Waitangi Tribunal can only suggest. It cannot make the government do as it suggests.

1 In the boxes write either PAKEHA, MAORI or WAITANGI TRIBUNAL to show which are most likely referred to.

	a used to own all the land of New Zealand
	b has heard hundreds of cases
	c had chiefs as leaders
	d checks out grievances
	e were members of tribes
	f is a special court
	g built up grievances
	h was created to do a special job
	i said the Treaty of Waitangi had been broken
	j can be members of the Waitangi Tribunal
	k brought British system of government to New Zealand
	l had land confiscated in the 1860s
	m had the Waitangi Tribunal set up for them
	n can only make suggestions
	o is an important culture in biculturalism
	p bought land when they came to New Zealand

9780170217804

Kiwi hero Sir Peter Blake

People admired Peter Blake because he was brave, a great planner and organiser, a leader, determined, a wonderful sailor, passionate about the environment, modest, down-to-earth and an inspiration to others.

During the 1995 America's Cup, Blake was the mainsail trimmer on the Kiwi boat. He wore the same pair of red socks. The only race the Kiwis lost was on the day Blake was rested. Before the final race, Kiwis bought tens of thousands of pairs of Blake's 'lucky red socks'.

1948	born in Auckland, New Zealand
1979	line honours and course record in Fastnet race
1980	line and handicap honours Sydney-Hobart race
1982	NZ's Yachtsman of the Year
1988	line honours in two-man round Australia race
1989/90	line, handicap and overall honours for round-the-world race
1989	NZ's Sports Personality of the Year
1990	NZ's Sportsman of the Year; NZ's Yachtsman of the Year
1994	Jules Verne Trophy for fastest non-stop circumnavigation of world; World Sailor of the Year; British Yachtsman of the Year
1995	head of NZ's America's Cup challenge; knighted (made a Sir)
1997	captain of Cousteau Society
2000	led NZ's successful America's Cup defence; set up *blakexpeditions* to teach people about environment
2001	*blakexpeditions* voyage to Antarctic; United Nations Environment Programme made him a special envoy; killed by pirates on a *blakexpeditions* voyage in Amazonia, Brazil; buried in England

1 Write the names of the following places connected to Peter Blake in the boxes on the map to show where they are.

a the country he was born in
b the country he was buried in
c the area *blakexpeditions* first voyaged to
d the country where the pirates who killed him came from
e the huge river his boat was anchored near when he was killed

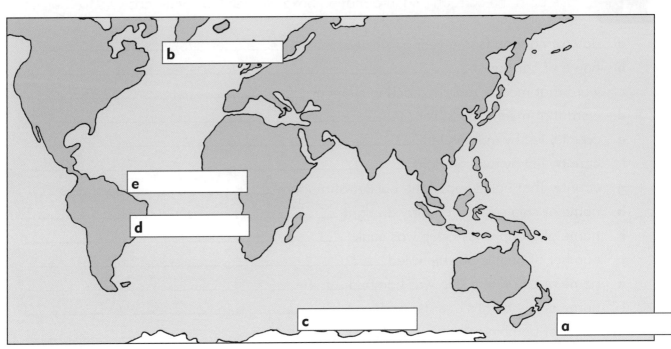

The sinking of the *Rainbow Warrior* in 1985

1 Greenpeace is angry at France testing nuclear bombs at Mururoa in South Pacific.

2 Greenpeace's ship *Rainbow Warrior* in Auckland Harbour gets ready to go to Mururoa to protest against nuclear testing.

3 French government plot code-named Operation Satanic plans to sink *Rainbow Warrior*.

4 French secret agents, posing as divers, came to NZ; used yacht to bring bombs (limpet mines), rubber dinghy, diving gear.

5 'Divers' meet up with another, two secret agents posing as honeymooners in a campervan; 'divers' hand over bombs and gear.

6 'Honeymooners' pass bombs and gear to special diving team.

7 Diving team attach two mines to *Rainbow Warrior*.

8 11.30 p.m. 10 July bombs explode; *Rainbow Warrior* sinks.

9 Photographer on board drowns.

10 Only agents that police find are the two 'honeymooners'; they get 10 years in prison.

11 The French are angry; they refuse to do some trade deals with NZ; many French say the agents' only sin is getting caught.

12 NZ gives in to pressure; releases the two agents to French.

13 France put agents on military base in French Polynesia.

14 France let agents go back home; agents are treated as heroes in France.

15 France agrees to pay $NZ13 million damages to NZ.

16 The wreck of *Rainbow Warrior* is taken to the Far North and sunk in a bay to make a recreational diving site.

1 Use both the cartoon and information boxes to help you write answers to the following:

a date of cartoon (same year as sinking) _____

b name of cartoonist _____

c word that means 'rude and acting superior' _____

d word that means 'possible' _____

e country led by man on left _____

f country led by man on right _____

g country that has dumped the bucket of manure _____

h name of ship sunk by country on right _____

i name of group whose ship was sunk _____

j number of people on ship killed _____

k name of city where ship was bombed _____

l name of the bombs agents used _____

m name of bombing plot _____

New Zealand's first America's Cup win in 1995

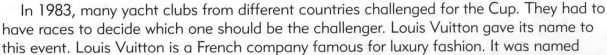

The America's Cup is the oldest sports trophy, continuously contested, in the world. It is sailing's greatest prize. Any country who wins it is looked up to by others.

The Cup is a very fancy silver pitcher. It was made in 1848 by Garrards the Crown Jewellers in London. People call it the Auld (Old) Mug.

The British put up the Cup as a challenge in 1851 for anyone to go for. The schooner *America* won it in a race against the Isle of Wight in England. The Americans took the trophy off to New York and named it The America's Cup. The New York Yacht Club kept winning the Cup after that.

In 1983, many yacht clubs from different countries challenged for the Cup. They had to have races to decide which one should be the challenger. Louis Vuitton gave its name to this event. Louis Vuitton is a French company famous for luxury fashion. It was named after the man who founded it. The winner of the Louis Vuitton Cup gets to race the America's Cup holder.

In 1995 Team New Zealand's NZL-32 *Black Magic* boat in San Diego in California had won the right to be the challenger for the America's Cup. There it thrashed Dennis Conner's boat *Young America* 5-0. Team New Zealand brought the Cup to Auckland. It won it by sailing magic, smart thinking, high technology and brilliant boat design.

It wasn't going to be the only time New Zealand won the Cup, but it was the first, so it was a special party time. Kiwis were overjoyed. There were huge street parades. The skipper Russell Coutts became a hero. New Zealand was the smallest country ever to take part in The America's Cup. And it had won.

In 1997 a Maori activist (someone who uses direct action for a political cause) attacked the Cup with a sledge-hammer. The Cup was badly damaged. The man was jailed. News of the attack flew around the world. Offers of help flooded in. Garrards offered to mend the Cup free of charge. It was a huge job. The mended Cup came back to New Zealand sitting in its own first-class plane seat.

---

 1 Write the events in the box into the boxes below, with their dates, to show in which order they happened.

> NZ won the Cup for the first time   Garrards mended the Cup
> Garrards made the Cup   The Louis Vuitton Cup was first raced for
> The Auld Mug was first raced for

a

b

c

d

e

UNIT 44

The Helen Years

The Helen Years refer to 1999 – 2008 when the Prime Minister (PM) of New Zealand, as leader of the Labour Party, was Helen Clark. She was the first female to hold the office by winning an election.

During this time an international survey put her in the Top 20 of The World's Most Powerful Women. Two months after she lost office, New Zealanders voted her the Greatest Living New Zealander.

As PM, Helen Clark won the UN Environment Programme Champions of the Earth for her government's work in sustainability – looking after the resources of the country such

as water and land so future generations would be able to also use them.

Helen Clark was also Minister for Arts, Culture and Heritage, involved in the New Zealand Security Intelligence Service and worked in many other areas such as being patron of New Zealand Rugby League.

In 2009 she was appointed Administrator of the United Nations Development Programme. She was the first female to lead this organisation, which works with a budget of billions of dollars to help people in need such as those in countries damaged by war, poverty and disease.

1 Use the photo to help name the following.

a the name of the city _____

b the name of the building/s _____

c the top job Helen Clark held there _____

d the number of years she held the top job _____

e the party she led _____

2 Give five examples that show Helen Clark achieved more than the average person.

a _____

b _____

c _____

d _____

e _____

9780170217804

New Zealand becomes Middle Earth

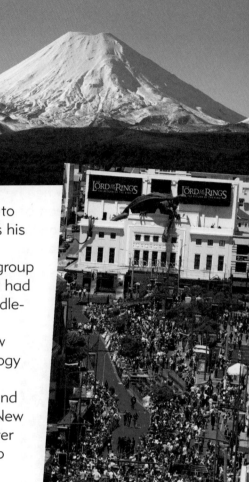

In the early 21st century New Zealand won hundreds of thousands of fans from all around the world. These fans learned where New Zealand was located in the world and many of them visited as tourists.

A trilogy of movies was the cause. Kiwi film-director Peter Jackson decided to film *The Lord of the Rings*, written by an Englishman called John Ronald Reuel Tolkien and published in the 1950s. Tolkien used Middle-earth, often now written as Middle Earth, to describe the lands of men. And Jackson used New Zealand as his Middle-earth.

The story is about a hobbit called Frodo who, with a small group of helpers, is on a quest to destroy the One Ring. A Dark Lord had created it at Mt Doom to get power over all the people of Middle-earth and it was the only place it can be destroyed.

However, in many ways the real star of the movies was New Zealand. As the publicity said, it took two years to film the trilogy but millions of years to build the sets.

Jackson's films were released in December of 2001, 2002 and 2003. Peter Jackson, the New Zealand film industry, and the New Zealand scenery became international super-stars. Jackson later became Sir Peter, and the movies won awards. People came to see places, such as Mt Doom (Mt Ngauruhoe). Thousands of overseas visitors now tread the same path as Frodo when they do the Tongariro Crossing, known to be one of the best one-day walks in the world.

World premiere of Lord of the Rings *in Wellington.*

> **1** Use the information above to help name the following.

a the real life mountain _____

b the movie mountain _____

c the hobbit who had to climb it _____

> **2** Give the main cause of New Zealand becoming Middle Earth.

_____

_____

> **3** Give three results of New Zealand becoming Middle Earth.

a _____

b _____

c _____

New Zealand's first VC

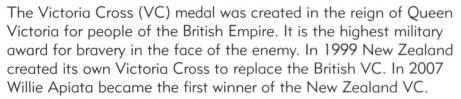

The Victoria Cross (VC) medal was created in the reign of Queen Victoria for people of the British Empire. It is the highest military award for bravery in the face of the enemy. In 1999 New Zealand created its own Victoria Cross to replace the British VC. In 2007 Willie Apiata became the first winner of the New Zealand VC.

Willie was born in Mangakino in Waikato in 1972. His mother was Pakeha and he was affiliated to Nga Puhi iwi through his Maori father. He went to school in Te Kaha. In 1989 he joined the New Zealand Army. Later he tried and failed to join the Special Air Service. He was successful when he tried again in 2001.

In 2004 he was part of an SAS troop in Afghanistan, fighting terrorism. One night in a rocky outback area about 20 enemy attacked with grenades, machine guns and automatic rifles. They destroyed a troop vehicle, put another out of action, and blew Willie Apiata off

the bonnet of the vehicle where he had been sleeping. One of two wounded soldiers had life-threatening bleeding. Willie Apiata took charge and decided all three of them had to rejoin the troop about 70 metres behind them. He then carried the bleeding soldier under fire not only from the enemy but also under returning fire from his troop. All three survived. Willie Apiata then re-armed and rejoined the battle. For this action he won the VC.

After the medal presentation at Government House in Wellington, Willie Apiata went to a homecoming ceremony held in Te Kaha. Later he donated all his medals, including his VC, to New Zealand. In a 2008 poll he was voted as 'The most trusted New Zealander'.

1 Use the photo of a typical patrol route in Afghanistan to help provide the following.

a one word to describe the road _____

b one word to describe the terrain (land) _____

c the reason Willie Apiata was there _____

d the group he belonged to _____

e what he did that won him the VC _____

2 Use the following description of a VC to colour it in.

ribbon = wine-red   cross = gunmetal grey

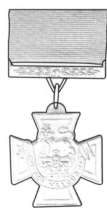

3 Give two actions Willie Apiata did after being presented with the VC.

a _____

b _____

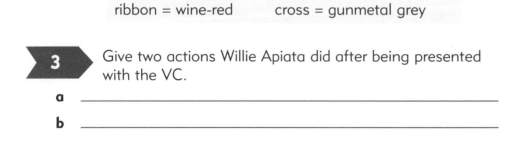

UNIT 47

All Whites make history

The soccer World Cup was held in South Africa from 11 June to 11 July 2010. It was the most-viewed sporting event in the world. Only 32 teams were chosen to play in it. New Zealand's team, the All Whites, made history through eight huge achievements.

Huge achievement 1: New Zealand qualified by beating Bahrain. This was only the second time in history that an All Whites team had qualified for the World Cup. Many people said the team was not good enough to be there.

Huge achievement 2: In their first game New Zealand drew 1-1 against Slovakia. This was the first time a Kiwi team had scored a point at World Cup level. It captured the attention of world media. New Zealanders sent messages of support.

Huge achievement 3: In their next game, New Zealand drew 1-1 against world champions Italy.

Huge achievement 4: In their last game, New Zealand drew 0-0 against group winners Paraguay to finish third in their group, ahead of Italy.

Huge achievement 5: Although New Zealand was then out of the Cup, it stayed the only unbeaten team there as the eventual winners had lost their opening game.

Huge achievement 6: New Zealand went to the Cup with a world ranking of 78. (Australia's ranking was 20 and Australia opened their World Cup with a 4-0 loss.) New Zealand's ranking soared up to 54. It finished the Cup ranked 22 out of the 32 teams. This put it ahead of giants like Italy and France.

Huge achievement 7: The All Whites skipper was named in the World Cup Best 11 picked by American sports television channel ESPN.

Huge achievement 8: A poll showed more than twice the number of people in New Zealand were interested in the All Whites' adventure than the All Blacks' tests.

1 Draw arrows to match countries to the following descriptions.

a Punched above its weight at the Cup.
b World Cup defending champions.
c Where the Cup took place.
d Along with Italy, considered a soccer giant.
e New Zealand beat them to qualify for the Cup.
f New Zealand played them in the first round.
g Opened campaign with a 4-0 loss.

AUSTRALIA
BAHRAIN
FRANCE
ITALY
NEW ZEALAND
SLOVAKIA
SOUTH AFRICA

2 State what each of the following figures refer to in relation to the Cup.

a 32 _____

b 22 _____

c 78 _____

d 54 _____

New Zealand's first Super City

Until 2010, Auckland was governed by eight separate councils. Many people felt this stopped Auckland progressing. Therefore on 1 November 2010 the eight councils merged into one super city and one mayor was elected for the whole area.

The first mayor, Len Brown, talked about Auckland:

- becoming the world's most livable city
- becoming an eco-city (one friendly to the environment)
- being a modern cruise-ship terminal
- having a low carbon future
- investigating solar energy
- having more affordable housing
- improving its waterways
- making sure there was plenty of surrounding green space
- building an excellent transport system such as rapid rail
- improving the education and skill levels of young people
- getting a good relationship between its people, environment and economy.

It is expected 75 percent of all the people in the world will live in cities by 2050. Over two and a half million will live in Auckland. When Auckland became a super city its population was already over 1.4 million.

In November 2010, Auckland contributed about 35 percent of NZ's annual GDP (Gross Domestic Product = the value of all the goods and services produced by a country). This made it one of just a few world cities that produced more than 30 percent of their country's GDP.

1 Use the photo to help name the following.

a the city _____

b the main natural feature shown _____

c the tallest manmade feature shown _____

d the year it became a super city _____

e the number of councils that merged together _____

f the type of city its mayor of the time wanted it to be _____

2 Give three examples of why Auckland is thought of as a leading city in New Zealand.

a _____

b _____

c _____

Pike River

COAL MINE DISASTERS IN NEW ZEALAND			
YEAR	MINE	LOCATION	DEATHS
1879	Kaitangata	Otago	34
1896	Brunner	West Coast	65
1914	Huntly	Waikato	43
1926	Dobson	West Coast	9
1939	Huntly	Waikato	11
1967	Strongman	West Coast	19
2010	Pike River	West Coast	29

The Pike River mine was to begin production in early 2008 and was expected to produce about one million tonnes of coal each year for about 20 years. This would have made it the largest underground coal mine in New Zealand. Delays meant the mining was not underway until the end of 2008 and production was slow.

From 19 – 28 November 2010 four explosions happened at the mine and trapped 29 miners inside. After the first explosion, experts said it would be several days before it was safe enough for rescue workers to enter. A major fear was the gases inside the mine would be explosive. The experts believed the explosion would have killed the trapped miners. They sent in two bomb disposal robots to check the situation but the second explosion stopped that effort.

On 2 December an official memorial service was held for the 29 miners, still inside the mine. The whole country united in mourning. The youngest miner had been on his first shift underground after celebrating his 17th birthday the day before.

In March 2011 Prince William visited Greymouth and met with families affected by the disaster.

> **1** Use the photo to help name the following.

a   the substance in the miner's hand _____

b   four places on the West Coast where this substance has been found

_____   _____   _____   _____

c   two ways a miner could be killed underground

_____

_____

> **2** Using the table (top right), put the name of the mining disaster in the box that it most likely represents.

Deaths in Mine Disasters

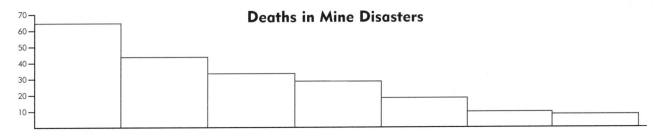

Magnitude: 6.3

Depth: 5 km

Time: 12.51 pm

Date: 22 February 2011

Epicentre: near Lyttelton, 10 km south-east of centre of Christchurch

Previous: 2010 September earthquake of magnitude 7.1 caused damage but no deaths

After-shocks: many hundreds e.g. 7 between 4pm on May 14 and 3pm on May 15 2011

Deaths: 181

Damage: buildings and infrastructure

Two major buildings: Christchurch Cathedral lost its spire; six-storey Canterbury Television (CTV) building collapsed and caught fire

Tsunami: 3.5 m tsunami waves in Tasman Lake after the quake caused glacier carving from Tasman Glacier

Ground: liquefaction; hundreds of thousands of tonnes of silt; surface flooding; landslides

Inner-city: red zone cordoned off from public

Sewage: major damage to sewer pipes and pump stations which sent untreated human sewage into rivers and beaches

Animals: some pets lost or upset

People: survivors traumatised; some evacuated, some left

Government reaction: responded immediately; a minister was freed up so he could concentrate solely on earthquake recovery; parliament adjourned and the PM and other ministers visited the area several times

Mayor: declared a state of emergency

Security: extra police called in

Fire Service: managed search and rescue

Sport: events cancelled e.g. Christchurch was to host some matches for the 2011 Rugby World Cup but these games were moved to other locations

Support from within New Zealand: organisations and groups e.g. Royal New Zealand Air Force, Defence Force, St John Ambulance, New Zealand Red Cross, Salvation Army, navy ship *Canterbury* in Lyttelton Harbour provided meals for homeless

9780170217804

Other countries: people from countries including Australia, Japan, US, UK, Taiwan and China sent in to help recovery

Fund-raising: set up throughout New Zealand; groups helped e.g. Foo Fighters held a Christchurch benefit concert in Auckland

Clean-up: thousands of people helped

Expense: New Zealand's most expensive natural disaster because of billions of dollars needed to rebuild

1 Find the words that mean the following.

a government can stop normal work and essential services _____

b officials moved people out of their houses _____

c stopped operating for a while _____

d shocked and not functioning normally _____

e services and facilities such as power _____

f sandy soil shaken violently causing water to rise up _____

2 Use the photo to help answer the following.

a Is there obvious liquefaction? _____

b What is the earliest date and time this photo could have been taken?

_____

c Is either the Christchurch Cathedral or the CTV building in this photo?

_____

d What is the reason for your answer to c? _____

New Zealand 100% Pure You

New Zealand's global tourism marketing campaign, `100% Pure New Zealand´, was launched in Queenstown in 1999. It was the first time New Zealand had a single tourism message that media could use and spread around the world. The 100% Pure campaign gave the idea that New Zealand was clean and green and tourists would get to see untouched and unspoiled environments.

A year later visitor numbers to New Zealand were up 10 percent and visitor spending was up 20 percent. Ten years later New Zealand was in top place of a survey by the United Nations asking what countries were best at destination branding.

In 2007, Tourism New Zealand launched a new era of the `100% Pure New Zealand´ advertising campaign, with a focus on New Zealand as the youngest country on Earth. The idea was that this youthfulness was unique to New Zealand and made its people and environments fresh and unspoilt. With the help of Weta Digital, Tourism New Zealand created a new television commercial featuring the Maori creation story and the North Island being fished up from the sea. The advertising campaign began with a 24-hour takeover of YouTube's global homepage.

2011 saw the launching of the `100% Pure You´ campaign. This new message aimed to personalise the New Zealand holiday experience for individuals and for countries. For example, marketing people knew that a major reason for Chinese tourists coming here is to be rejuvenated. So the advertising campaign line in China said 'New Zealand 100% revives you'. For the US and Canada it was `New Zealand never leaves you´; for the UK it was 'New Zealand, it's about time'. In France it was 'New Zealand has the holiday for you' and in Germany it was 'Discover New Zealand'. All these messages were combined with showing what different experiences individuals could have in a stunning environment.

The brand had its critics, both inside and outside of New Zealand, who pointed out that New Zealand was not actually 100 percent clean and green. Defenders of the brand said New Zealand had a cleaner and greener environment than most other countries, and was working hard to fix problems, such as preserving its endangered species.

YOU COULD BE FLYING TO THE MOST RELAXING HOLIDAY EVER. OR THE MOST EXCITING.

Whatever you enjoy, one place on earth has your ideal holiday. Discover the escape that's just perfect for you. **Visit newzealand.com today.**

NEW ZEALAND 100% PURE

newzealand.com

1 Give two words that images such as the one above are supposed to suggest to tourists about New Zealand.

a _____

b _____

2 Give the major focus this image would have been part of in the following years.

a 1999 _____

b 2007 _____

c 2011 _____

3 Give the link between tourism marketing and the following.

a Queenstown _____

b YouTube _____

c Weta Digital _____

d the Maori creation story _____

e 'Discover New Zealand' _____

f China _____

g Canada _____

h UK _____

i France _____

4 How do defenders of the New Zealand clean and green image defend it against critics?

_____

_____

Just a few reasons why New Zealand is special

It's staunch
Many people on both sides of the Tasman thought New Zealand should join as the seventh state when the six colonies of Australia joined together in 1901 to become the federation of Australia. But it said no.

Its leaders make a splash
An example was Richard John Seddon who became Premier in 1893. 'King Dick' weighed about 127 kg. He often behaved as if New Zealand was the centre of the whole world.

It's smart
It has produced famous writers. Examples are the short story writer Katherine Mansfield who was born in 1888, and Keri Hulme who won the Booker Prize in 1985 for her novel *The Bone People*.

It's female-friendly
In 1999 Helen Clark became its first elected female Prime Minister. In 2001 its PM, leader of the opposition (she lost her job later), Attorney-General, Chief Justice and Governor-General were all female.

It's unbiased
It was the first country in the world to elect a transsexual as a mayor. It was also the first country in the world to elect a transsexual (the same person) as a member of Parliament. A transsexual is a person who has changed sex.

It's funky
An example is its Wearable Art Awards, which were first held in 1987 in Nelson. The aim was to take art off the walls and put it on the body beautiful in wild and wacky ways.

Its movies are famous
Examples: Kiwi director Peter Jackson began filming *The Hobbit* in 2011. In 1993 Kiwi movie *The Piano* won Oscars for 11-year-old Kiwi actress Anna Paquin, and Kiwi Jane Campion for screenplay.

It's sporty
Example: Kiwi Anthony Wilding was the best tennis player in the world. He played tennis in long trousers and a long-sleeved shirt. He kept winning singles and doubles at Wimbledon but was killed in 1915 during World War 1.

It's responsible
Example: In 1999 New Zealand sent peace-keeping troops into East Timor which was a big trouble-spot. It offered to join in the world fight against terrorism when terrorists attacked the US in 2001.

2011 Brancott Estate WOW Awards Show

It's fair
Example: New Zealand worked hard to get human rights put on the agenda when the United Nations was being set up at the end of World War 2. This was when other countries didn't at first want to know about human rights.

It's brave

Example: New Zealand wasn't scared to go against the USA by having an anti-nuclear policy. This led it to refuse a visit by an American warship in 1985 because the US wouldn't say if the ship was nuclear or not.

It's green

Example: New Zealand is famous for having many national parks. Its first national park was Tongariro. It was set up 1887. It was given to the nation by Te Heuheu Tukino IV.

It's travel-friendly

Example: its first car was imported in 1898. The Auckland-to-Wellington main trunk railway opened in 1908. The first plane flight across Cook Strait took place in 1920.

It's a great host

Example: the Commonwealth Games of 1990 were held in Auckland. They were known as the High-Tech Games. In 1999 Auckland hosted a big world leaders' conference. The American President came to it. In 2011 New Zealand hosted the Rugby World Cup.

> **1** Finish the time line by writing in the missing information.

DATE	EVENT
_____	first national park
1888	_____
_____	Seddon became Premier
1898	_____
_____	New Zealand refused to join Australia
1908	_____
_____	death of Anthony Wilding
_____	American warship refused entry
1985	_____
_____	first Wearable Art Awards
1990	_____
_____	Anna Paquin's Oscar
_____	first elected female PM
1999	_____
_____	Kiwi troops sent to East Timor
_____	New Zealand hosts the Rugby World Cup

1   Tangata whenua means people of the _____.

2   The Polynesian who is said to have visited NZ in 925 was called

     _____.

3   Hawaiki is the name given to the ancient _____ of
     ancestors of the Maori.

4   The Great Fleet Theory said eight _____ came to NZ in
     1350.

5   Abel Tasman saw New Zealand in the _____ century.

6   Tasman came from the country of _____.

7   Zeeland was an area in the country of _____.

8   James Cook came from the country of _____.

9   Cook made his crew eat fruit and greens to stop them getting the disease of

     _____.

10   The name of Cook's ship that sailed right around New Zealand was

     _____.

11   The Treaty of Waitangi was signed in the year _____.

12   The name of the person who signed the treaty for the Crown was

     _____.

13   The group of people who signed the treaty for Maori were the

     _____.

14   'He iwi tahi tatou' means in English _____

15   The two languages that the treaty was written in are _____ and

     _____.

16   'Not all tribes signed the Treaty of Waitangi.' Is that true OR false?

     _____

17   In the 1840s a ship took four to six _____ to get from Britain to
     NZ.

18   The name of the chief responsible for the flagpole chopping was

     _____.

19   Maori chopped down the flagpole _____ times.

20   Chief Kawiti was very good at _____ and he made Maori pa much
     stronger.

21   The first Maori king, Te Wherowhero, was a chief from

     _____.

22   A tohunga is a Maori _____.

23   In 1966 Te Atairangikaahu became the first Maori _____.

24   Maori tribes did not own land as individuals but as _____.

25   The wars of the 1860s were fought in the _____ Island.

9780170217804

26 Trenches built for British soldiers to get close to Maori pa were called _____.

27 During the 1860s, the government confiscated Maori _____.

28 The biggest gold mine, the Martha Hill mine, is at _____ in the Coromandel.

29 Gabriel Read was the first to find _____ in Otago.

30 By the 1870s only _____ in the lower North Island was left to make farms.

31 The Buried Village was buried by the eruption of Mt _____ in 1886.

32 Te _____ was the leader of the Parihaka village.

33 Parihaka was near the mountain called _____.

34 The white feather of the _____ was the emblem for Parihaka.

35 The ship that took the first frozen meat to London in 1882 was called _____.

36 The Boer War took place in the country of _____.

37 Boers were people who originally came from the country of _____.

38 The Kiwi soldiers in the Boer War got the nickname of Rough _____.

39 In the 19th century, school students had to write on small boards called _____.

40 Another term for a shanghai is a _____.

41 Suffrage and franchise are other words for _____.

42 The first country in the world to give women the vote was _____.

43 A pension is a regular payment of money by _____ to the needy.

44 In 1898 parliament passed a law to give _____ pensions.

45 In 1905 a NZ team that came to be called the _____ toured Britain.

46 The 1915 Anzacs took part in the _____ campaign against the Turks.

47 Calling men up to fight is called c_____.

48 In 1918 there was a big _____ epidemic.

49 A drop in business activity causing mass unemployment is called a _____.

50 Richard Pearse and Jean Batten were famous early _____.

51 The name of the man who split the atom is _____.

52 The British abbey where this man is buried is called _____.

53 The 1936 Olympics were held in the German city of _____.

54 The name of the leader of Germany at that time was _____.

55 The name of the man who won NZ's first Olympic track gold medal is
    _____.

56 The city where the Centennial Exhibition of 1939–40 was held was
    _____.

57 World War 2 started in the year _____.

58 Winston Churchill was the Prime Minister of _____
    during World War 2.

59 Michael Savage was _____ of NZ when World War 2
    started.

60 Did any NZ soldiers fight to keep Greece and Crete free of the Nazis?
    _____

61 Thousands of servicemen from the country of _____ spent time in NZ in World
    War 2.

62 The medal won by Charles Upham and Te Moananui a Kiwa Ngarimu is the
    _____.

63 In 1945 the US dropped atomic bombs on the country of _____.

64 Mt Everest is part of a great mountain chain called the
    _____.

65 The name of the Kiwi who first climbed Mt Everest is _____.

66 The British Royal who was crowned in 1953 was _____.

67 Selwyn Toogood's radio and TV show was called It's in the
    _____.

68 The new money system that started in 1967 is called _____.

69 The new entertainment of the 1960s that put many movie theatres out of business is
    called _____.

70 A harbour bridge was built in 1959 in the city of _____.

71 The English word for the Maori word hikoi is _____.

72 People on the 1975 hikoi walked from the Far North to
    _____.

73 Peter Blake's good luck charm in the 1995 America's Cup was
    _____.

74 Joe Hawke led a protest in 1977 at _____ Point.

75 A nine-year-old girl died in a _____ during the protest at Bastion
    Point.

76 Whina Cooper was called the _____ of the Nation.

77 Mt Erebus is situated at the _____ Pole.

78 The name of NZ's base at Antarctica is _____ Base.

79 The South African animal that gives its name to their rugby team is
    _____.

80 The system of race laws that South Africa had in 1981 was called
    _____.

81 The name of the giant in the ancient story who had to hold the heavens on his
    shoulders was _____.

82 In 1975 the government set up the _____ Tribunal to
    hear Maori grievances.

83 In the 1970s the government made Waitangi Day a national
    _____.

84 Biculturalism is when _____ cultures are made equally important.

85 The ship *Rainbow Warrior* belonged to the _____ organisation.

86 The *Rainbow Warrior* was sunk by secret agents from the country of _____.

87 The skipper of *Black Magic* in 1995 was _____.

88 Which country might NZ have joined in 1901? _____

89 Premier Richard Seddon's nickname was _____.

90 The kind of literature Katherine Mansfield is famous for is _____.

91 The director of the *Lord of the Rings* movie trilogy is _____.

92 The sport that Anthony Wilding became famous for is _____.

93 Tongariro was the first National _____ to be set up.

94 The first _____ was imported and driven in 1898.

95 The city of _____ was the first to host the Wearable Art Awards.

96 NZ refused to let a warship from the country of _____ visit in 1985.

97 Danyon Loader won Olympic golds in the sport of _____.

98 The America's Cup was attacked with a sledgehammer in 1997 by a _____.

99 Into which country did NZ send peace-keeping troops in 1999? _____.

100 In 2001 NZ offered to help in the global fight against _____.

/100

Bonus Points: Who are these people?

a

_____
_____

b

_____
_____

c

_____
_____

d

_____
_____

e

_____
_____

f

_____
_____

g

_____
_____

h

_____
_____

/8